To Samue[l]
Thanks for [it]
Spend time c/ your family,
Blessings on your Home!

Finances:
Biblical Wisdom/Radical Action

Managing Your Financial and Business Concerns

By Dr. Dow Pursley
and
Gordon Puls

Copyright 05/2011
Revised 07/2016

ISBN: 978-1-5333-0886-3

This book is not for sale.

This book along with Radical Heart/Radical Marriage are both available for download or purchase on kindle or online. To receive a free book copy it is available on createspace.com. To receive a kindle reader copy it can be found under free books on Amazon.com, however there is a modest processing fee from kindle.

Sincerely,

Dr. Dow Pursley and Gordon Puls

Financial Management
Copyright © 2011 by Dr. Dow Pursley
Revised 2016
ISBN: 978-1-5333-0886-3

Requests for information should be addressed to:

Alethia Publishing House   Editorial Vida & Esperanza
15358 Twin Pines Rd.   CC La Rotonda II – 2052
Lowell, Ar. 72745   Av. La Fontana 440 La Molina
                                 Lima 12, Peru

Library of Congress Cataloging-in-Publication Data
Pursley, Dow
    Financial Management: Biblical Wisdom/Radical Action—
Financial Decision Making That Affects Your Life, Dow Pursley
and Gordon Puls

Unless otherwise noted, all quotes from the Bible are from the
thought for thought translation of The Living Bible, Copyright
©1971 by Tyndale House Publishers, Inc. Wheaton, Illinois

Cover Design by Dawn Jacobs

This book is dedicated to my wife, Joanne, who has always been supportive of my ventures and a great partner in marriage and business.

Dr. Dow Pursley

Contents

Preface

I had the great privilege of owning and operating several businesses during the course of my life. Whatever success I have had, I owe it to the Lord of the Proverbs. There were also several men who mentored me in the practice of business, some of whom I mention by name and others by stories in this book. Tony Butts from South Africa, the maize-producing giant of Zambia and Zimbabwe; small businessman James Beavers; the late Mr. Larry Burkett of Larry Burkett Ministries; Mr. Rick Parsons and his gracious father, who allowed a small group of businessmen to come to breakfast at their home weekly and learn the principles of Crown Ministries; Mr. and Mrs. Love and Philip and Becky Elder-Love of the Love-Box Company of Wichita, Kansas, who have exemplified Christ in their personal and business life.

I had the honor of being mentored by Ed Wheat, M.D. I worked as a colleague with him and experienced one of the warmest and most significant friendships a person can have in life. Ed Wheat was one of those rare men who, after his conversion at age thirty-eight, applied his intellect to the study of the Scriptures and became a biblical scholar. Dr. Wheat used his medical knowledge as a platform to share the Gospel with all of his patients. With the use of his medical skills, he and his wife, Gaye Wheat, wrote his first book, *Intended for Pleasure*.

I was honored to write chapter ten in Dr. Wheat's book, *Secret Choices*, and to expand his work, *Intended for Pleasure*, and a study guide for *Love-Life for Every Married Couple* also by Ed Wheat, M.D. The Lord was pleased to take His servant, Ed Wheat, home in September of 2001. Although he is greatly missed, heaven is richer.

I am currently retired after serving as a professor in the Graduate School, and the Director of Clinical Programs at

Clark Summit University, Seminary and Graduate School located at
538 Venard Rd., Clarks Summit, PA 18411. Phone: 1-800-451-7664, Fax: (570) 585-9305, Graduate School: (570) 585-9349, Love-Life Marriage and Family Center: (570) 585-9415 or email Dr. Pursley at combatkarate@aol.com.

We are pleased to announce the opening of The Love-Life Marriage and Family Center on the campus of Clark Summit University and Seminary. Here, we counsel couples and
families with the biblical methods and principles that Dr. Wheat carefully mined from the wealth of God's Word. We train our graduate students here at the campus with practical, hands-on counseling experience, under supervision.

Special thanks are in order for the preparation, editing, typing, and consultation of this manual. The initial editing was accomplished by a former professor, colleague and friend, Gordon Puls, the smartest man I know. As with so many works, others have helped in the editing process for the final draft. Special thanks goes to Debbie Nichols, who always finds time to help me using her editing expertise, and Dawn Jacobs who brought this book to completion, which is greatly appreciated. Finally, thanks to my wife, Joanne, for her suggestions, insights and editing of the final draft.

Dr. Dow R. Pursley

Preface for the second edition

What an economic disaster we have left generations X, Y, Z, and Alpha. Why are people always trying things that have never worked in the past?

The Puritan economic experiments almost killed– for a people of the Book to choose Thomas Aquinas and "socialist" economics for the New World instead of actually going to the only source of the truth.

Well we have moved way past the mistakes the puritans made, so many trillions of dollars in debt and in the and in the midst of a failing global economy with neither any hope for moving forward or back to some distant past. No economy uses real money – the coins have been so degraded that some countries like Turkey decided to include counterfeited money into their economy.

With the problems we have left our future generations they will be forced to print their account numbers on their wrists or forehead to keep identity theft from taking place. Those who fear that much government interference in their lives and chips inserted in their bodies may be forced to barter and stay off the grid until they are apprehended and reeducated.

Is it possible to recover this financial global disaster? I have my doubts, but doing the right thing is the only way to proceed. I only hope the future generations will analyze how we left them with this mess and be willing to sacrifice and stop the free stuff nonsense and get rid of the blood suckers at the top and replace them with people like those who sacrificed their wealth, their lives, and their sacred honor. Go back to real money and see that biblical principles actually work.

"If a man doesn't work neither shall he eat"! Real Big changes that will anger an entitled generation but be a good start for those with biblical integrity while the blood sucking bottom fish that run this country do their own fishing.

Introduction

Oh how the "Mighty" has fallen, it has fallen.
Revelation 18:2

"In Times Like These...."

An old gospel song includes the line, "In times like these, we need an anchor." Imagery from the days of sailing ships is no longer used in casual conversation, but many of us know what it means to be caught in a storm of economic uncertainty. We long for a home port where we can find a "haven of rest," a place of security and peace, sheltered from the waves of adversity. We want an anchor that holds in the storms of life, keeping us from being tossed about by shifting markets and avarice of men. We need to know that we are not headed for ultimate shipwreck. In times like these, we need something more reliable than "business as usual."

"Business as usual" is, in fact, an obsolete expression. When the Soviet Union disintegrated, Western capitalists celebrated the failure of communism. More recently, there have been serious public discussions of the possible failure of capitalism. Government bailouts, massive fraud, global economic uncertainty—if "business as usual" created such a crisis, it would be irrational to believe that the common wisdom of financial wizards and the common practices of entrepreneurs can bring a return to relative economic stability. Governments, corporations, investors, and consumers are questioning the very foundations of "business as usual."

Businesses and business schools are being forced to consider matters of accountability—stockholders, customers, and governments are keeping a closer watch over how business is conducted. Accepted practices are being scrutinized for their legal viability, and even for their basic morality. Seminars and college courses are grasping for a consensus on complicated ethical issues.

It is not naïve to speak of faith-based ethics. Unless there is a God whose character defines what is right and what is wrong, there is no reliable standard—ethics and morality fall to the lowest common denominator within the dominant culture. Whatever works is right, as long as you don't get caught.

This book presents a faith-based approach to business ethics. "When all else fails, read the directions." It is becoming clear that all else has failed. It's time to read the directions—the Word of God.

Biblical Wisdom

Another old song says, "We have an anchor that keeps the soul steadfast and sure while the billows roll."Faith in God is not an escapist delusion, but the realistic foundation for a satisfying life. God's Word brings God's truth into the world's confusion. Although several generations have been absolutely certain that there are no absolutes, their experience proves them absolutely wrong. God is God, and what He says is absolutely true—and it works.

The Bible has answers to the questions men have about their lives and how to conduct themselves properly. The wisest and wealthiest man who ever lived (yes, even wealthier than Bill Gates!) wrote Proverbs. These statements of general truth about life are still true. Beginning with a right relationship with God, biblical proverbs help us know how to live with integrity. They are not a get-rich-quick scheme or a guarantee of great wealth; they are guidelines for solid, secure achievement. The biblical book of Proverbs does not stand alone; it is rooted in the wisdom of God, and interconnected with revelations of God's wisdom woven through the whole Bible. Beginning from the Proverbs, we can trace God's wisdom concerning financial management throughout the Scriptures. This biblical wisdom has led some successful business people to radical action, giving exemplary evidence that what God says works when all worldly wisdom fails. Why not listen to some common sense? The practical wisdom on these pages will have profound effects on your life, financial, and business practices.

The book of Proverbs begins with a call to see ourselves and our position in the world correctly. "The fear of the Lord," reverence for God and submission to His will, is referred to repeatedly as the basis for wisdom, contentment, and avoidance of evil. "To hear wisdom," listening to and following instruction and advice, is presented as the basis for living sensibly and successfully.

Radical Action

Faith is not fatalism. Trusting the God of the Bible includes obeying the commands of the Bible. "Trust and Obey" was another favorite in old hymnals. Historically, faith-based ethics were once the only ethics in use. Societies and individuals functioned under the "ethos," the unquestioned cumulative wisdom and practice of the community — almost invariably dictated by a common religion. Followers of Jesus Christ, then, may be expected to follow Jesus Christ in all aspects of their lives. For people of faith, faith-based ethics is not one option among many. Their ethics, whether at home or in the marketplace, are simply an expression of their faith.

Business practices which express one's faith are in some respects radically different from business practices which express one's greed. Self-interest, enlightened by social conscience or not, falls short of God's intentions for humanity. God Himself is actively and extravagantly benevolent. Does God help those who help themselves? Yes, in the sense that we must be active in carrying out His purposes. God also helps those who do not "help themselves," those who subordinate their self-interest to His glory. God definitely helps those who help others — whatever He gives us is intended for use in ministry.

Knowing God equips believers not only for "spiritual" ministry, but also for practical usefulness. Calvinists speak of "the Creation mandate" which calls us to use our gifts and opportunities to bring order and beauty to the world. Luther emphasized "vocation," our place and occupation in the world, with responsibilities to be fulfilled conscientiously and diligently. God gives each of His children unique abilities and opportunities which He empowers us to use to His glory. We will not all become wealthy in material goods, but we can all be wise in handling what God has given us.

Psalm 37 deals with the perennial question, "Why do the wicked prosper" (Jeremiah 12:1)? Many followers of Christ might well ask, "Why do some of the righteous prosper?" Some of us have not prospered by the world's standards. Jeremiah laments, "You have made us refuse and garbage among the nations" (Lamentations 3:45). Paul adds, "…we have gone hungry and thirsty, without even enough clothes to keep us warm. We have been kicked around without homes of our own. We have worked wearily with our hands to earn our living…. Yet right up to the present moment we are like dirt underfoot, like garbage" (I Corinthians 4:11-13). The material circumstances of believers vary as widely as those of non-believers—but our trust in God brings contentment as we live in obedient faith. The promises of the Proverbs are not slogans which guarantee unlimited material success. They must be read, and followed, in the context of the total message of the Bible.

Beginning from the Proverbs, we can connect to the wisdom of the whole Bible, and draw inferences and applications for the challenges our own time and place. Biblical wisdom teaches consistent principles for productive, satisfying life in conformity to God's purposes for His Creation. These principles have direct relevance to every decision we make and every action we take.

Conviction

What we believe defines who we are.

Most people do not examine the underlying assumptions by which they live. Yet differences in what we believe about God, the universe, and ourselves are fundamental to differences in our character and conduct. "The fear of the Lord" is the root assumption of the people of God. Reverent consciousness of the presence of God in our lives motivates us to seek His guidance and approval. Believing that God exists, and that His character determines what is right and wrong, we seek to understand and live out His purposes for our lives.

People without the fear of the Lord assume that they are autonomous, free to make up their own rules as they go along. Individually and corporately, they do what is right in their own eyes (Judges 21:25). Their consciences, character, and conduct are attuned to what works, what feels good, or what the market will stand, rather than to any fixed moral standard. When self-interest and unrestrained egotism become the primary motivating forces in a society, it becomes countercultural to commit ourselves to living our lives according to the Word of God. Yet that is the core identity of the believer — one who believes that God lives, and that He is present and active in our world.

Conviction? No, not in the legal sense of being declared guilty by a judge or jury, although that has happened to some people who thought they knew how to handle finances. As an ethical or religious term, "conviction" refers to a deeply held belief, or to a deeply felt stirring of the conscience. As the dominant culture privatizes matters of belief and conscience, business goes on without them. "The bottom line" takes precedence over high ideals. Lowering standards to raise profits is perceived as good business sense. People who start with

17

little or no conviction in the ethical or religious sense may find themselves with a conviction in the legal sense.

Biblical wisdom begins with foundational beliefs, and follows the dictates of a conscience informed by the Word of God. Conventional wisdom follows the rules of the market, and looks for new rules when the market fails. God's people start with the firm conviction that they represent God in all that they do. A faith-based approach to business ethics must begin with the fundamental beliefs which shape the conscience of a person of faith. For Christians, this is found in the teachings of the Bible.

The Fear of the Lord

The book of Proverbs makes explicit what much of biblical teaching assumes: we live our lives in the presence of the living God, whose character determines what is right and wrong. Out of reverence for God, we examine His written revelation of Himself in order to conform ourselves to His will. We presuppose that our Creator knows how His Creation is supposed to work, and that it is most reasonable to do things His way.

If God is really present and active in the world, and if He has spoken, our reasonable response is to find out what He has said, and make it the rule of our lives. Who is God? Who am I? What is God doing? What does He want me to do? A person who professes faith in the God of the Bible can be expected to live by the teachings of the Bible.

Faith-based ethics must begin with faith. God reveals Himself as "I am," the self-existing, self-sufficient One. Our first response must be reverent awe.

According to Proverbs—

- 1:7   *How does a man become wise? The first step is to trust and reverence the Lord!*

Only a fool would say to himself, 'There is no God (Psalm 53:1).'" "You can never please God without faith, without depending on him (Hebrews 11:6)." "Claiming themselves to be wise without God, they became utter fools instead (Romans 1:22)." The only true wisdom is God's wisdom. The way to know true wisdom is to know God. Excluding God from a search for wisdom is delusional, trying to frame an understanding of reality while excluding its source.

- 3:19   *The Lord's wisdom founded the earth; His understanding established all the universe and space.*

"Yes, I [wisdom] was born before God made the earth and fields, and high plateaus. I was there when He established the heavens and formed the great springs in the depths of the oceans. I was there when He set the limits of the seas and gave them His instructions not to spread beyond their boundaries. I was there when He made the blueprint for the earth and oceans (Proverbs 8:26-29)." "Since earliest times men have seen the earth and sky and all God made, and have known of his existence and great eternal power (Romans 1:20)." "The heavens are telling the glory of God; they are a marvelous display of his craftsmanship (Psalm 19:1)." The God whose wisdom brought all Creation into existence can be trusted to teach His creatures how to live.

The fear of the Lord recognizes the supremacy of the Creator over His Creation. As creatures, it is wise to seek the Creator's purpose for bringing us into existence, and to follow His design for our lives. As beings created in the image of God, it is wise for us to seek to know God well, and to conform to His character.

- 14:26   *Reverence for God gives a man deep strength; his children have a place of refuge and security.*

"For the eyes of the Lord search back and forth across the whole earth, looking for people whose hearts are perfect toward him, so that he can show his great power in helping them (II Chronicles 16:9)." "He will give his people strength. He will bless them with peace (Psalm 29:11)." Knowing God and following His wisdom establishes His people in quiet confidence and settled contentment. A home with this foundation is strengthened against the chaotic confusion of the godless world.

• 14:27 *Reverence for the Lord is a fountain of life; its waters keep a man from death.*

"The Lord is my light and my salvation; whom shall I fear (Psalm 27:1)?" "For you are the Fountain of life; our light is from your Light. Pour out your unfailing love on those who know you! Never stop giving your salvation to those who long to do your will (Psalm 66:9-10)." God's blessings upon His people sustain them in all circumstances.

Since God created us to be conformed to His image, strength and contentment come to those who live according to God's wisdom. Just as wise builders carefully follow blueprints, wise people carefully follow God's revelation of His purpose for our lives.

• 16:20 *God blesses those who obey Him; happy the man who trusts in the Lord.*

"There will be blessing if you obey the commandments of the Lord your God…, and a curse if you refuse them…. (Deuteronomy 11:27-28)." "Obey me and I will be your God and you shall be my people; only do as I say and all shall be well (Jeremiah 7:23)." "Obedience is better than sacrifice… (I Samuel 15:22)." Obeying God conforms our lives to the way Creation is meant to work, and brings the added blessing of pleasing our Creator. Obedience in the details of everyday decision-making demonstrates our faith more accurately than public performances of worship.

• 19:23 *Reverence for God gives life, happiness, and protection from harm.*

"We live in the shadow of the Almighty; sheltered by the God who is above all gods…. For Jehovah is my refuge! I choose the God above all gods to shelter me. How then can evil overtake me or any plague come near (Psalm 91:1, 9-10)?" Consciously and constantly choosing to live in obedient faith brings constant consciousness of God's presence and loving care.

The fear of the Lord recognizes God's presence in our lives, and submits to His direction. When we join God in carrying out His plans, our interests are bound up in His interests. Wanting what God wants brings us into partnership with God. Bringing God glory as we live out His character and plans, we find security and contentment that cannot be known in any other way.

• 20:24 *Since the Lord is directing our steps, why try to understand everything that happens along the way?*

"What you ought to say is, 'If the Lord wants us to, we shall live and do this or that.' Otherwise you will be bragging about your own plans, and such self-confidence never pleases God (James 4:15-16)." "We should make plans — counting on God to direct us (Proverbs 16:9)." Worldly wisdom teaches that street smarts and business sense will bring success to the shrewd and powerful. God's wisdom teaches that our best plans and most diligent efforts still leave God in control of the outcome.

• 21:2 *We can justify our every deed but God looks at our motives.*

"You must actively obey him in everything he commands. Only then will you be doing what is right and good in the Lord's eyes (Deuteronomy 6:17-18)." "You will no longer go your own way, everyone doing whatever he thinks is right (Deuteronomy 12:8)." Our motives are either godly or selfish. If we know and trust God, we will do what He says because it brings Him honor. If we are motivated by self-interest, we will do what brings benefits to ourselves, with or without considering the benefit or harm to others. "Let conscience be your guide" is not a safe option, because our consciences may be distorted or hardened by habitual rejection of God's wisdom. (Titus 1:15; I Timothy 4:2).

God is God; we are not. Our attempts to understand past experience or to predict the outcome of future actions fall short of God's wisdom. We want to make sense of the puzzling details of our lives, but worldly wisdom cannot make all the pieces fit. We are not in control—we are not the masters of our own fate. With God in control, we can find purpose and satisfaction. Without God, we face frustration and judgment.

- 22:4 *True humility and respect for the Lord lead a man to riches, honor and long life.*

"If you will humble yourselves under the mighty hand of God, in his good time he will lift you up (I Peter 5:6)." "Don't be impatient for the Lord to act! Keep traveling steadily along his pathway and in due season he will honor you with every blessing (Psalm 37:34)." There is no "get-rich-quick" scheme for the child of God. Our hope is to get blessed patiently.

- 28:14 *Blessed is the man who reveres God, but the man who doesn't care is headed for serious trouble.*

"I will bring evil upon this people; it will be the fruit of their own sin, because they will not listen to me (Jeremiah 6:19)." "God shows his anger from heaven against all sinful, evil men who push the truth away from them (Romans 1:18)." "But they that wait upon the Lord shall renew their strength. They shall mount up with wings like eagles; they shall run and not be weary, they shall walk and not faint (Isaiah 40:31)." Those who exclude God from their thoughts are doomed to failure and judgment. If we want to soar with the eagles, we must be heavenly minded, we must walk with God.

The fear of the Lord puts us in tune with the harmony God built into Creation. When God is in control, all things work together for our good (Romans 8:28). When we try to be autonomous, self-rule leads to self-destruction.

- 29:25 *Fear of man is a dangerous trap, but to trust in God means safety.*

"Stay away from the love of money; be satisfied with what you have. For God has said, 'I will never, never fail you nor forsake you.' That is why we can say without doubt or fear, 'The Lord is my Helper and I am not afraid of anything that mere man can do to me (Hebrews 13:5-6).'" Biblical witnesses followed God even when threatened with imprisonment or death (Acts 4:19-20; Daniel 3:16-18). Following God also means resisting peer pressure, and getting out of the boxes our culture creates for us: "Don't copy the behavior and customs of this world, but be a new and different person with a fresh newness in all you do and think. Then you will learn from your own experience how his [God's] ways will really satisfy you (Romans 12:2)."

• 30:5-6 *Every word of God proves true. He defends all who come to Him for protection. Do not add to His words, lest He rebuke you, and you be found a liar.*

"The whole Bible was given to us by inspiration from God and is useful to teach us what is true and to make us realize what is wrong in our lives; it straightens us out and helps us do what is right (II Timothy 3:16)." "God is not a man, that he should lie; He doesn't change his mind like humans do. Has he ever promised, without doing what he said (Numbers 23:19)?" "God's truth stands firm like a great rock, and nothing can shake it (II Timothy 2:19)." God's wisdom is the final authority for God's people; it overrules and excludes any so-called worldly wisdom which contradicts it.

The fear of man motivates us to conform to worldly wisdom, cultural norms which vary with time and place. The fear of the Lord motivates us to conform the God's wisdom, which never changes.

The fear of the Lord is the very opposite of abject terror. There is quiet confidence in knowing that the Creator of the Universe is present and active in our lives. The old Sunday school song may have frightened children when they were warned, "Be careful little hands what you do...." God is, in fact, watching the wicked closely, and will bring just judgment upon their evil deeds. But many children missed the comforting thought in the song—"the Father up above is looking down in love." God delights in His children, and looks out for their best interests. When God's children realize that their best interest is to glorify God, they have a healthy fear of doing anything which would compromise His plan for their lives. Their reverent awe of God motivates them to obedient faith. This "fear of the Lord" drives His people into His Word to find and follow His wisdom.

Wisdom

What is wisdom? In the comic strips, it's a punch line delivered by an old man on a mountaintop. In the movies, it's a bittersweet quip about lessons learned from harsh experience. At the senior center, it's nostalgic conversation about what could have been or should have been. At the bar or the beauty salon, it's unsolicited advice from unqualified sympathizers. Of course, none of these give us what we are really looking for when we want reliable counsel.

Popular parodies of wisdom do, however, bear some elements of truth. The man on the mountaintop is "above it all" and should be able to see "the big picture"—wisdom is an objective view of a situation, free of the irrational hopes and fears of participants in a particular struggle. The moral observation tagged onto the end of a movie is an attempt to make sense of a seemingly senseless world—wisdom is a summary of principles which seem to explain or predict the outcomes of common human experiences. Sadly, as the saying goes, senior citizens know that we get old too soon and wise too late—wisdom is mature judgment unblurred by the passion of the moment or the haziness of hindsight. Bartenders and hairdressers offer a forum for unguarded exposure of need and expression of opinion—wisdom is a nugget of truth which speaks precisely to a specific problem.

So where can we find real wisdom? Who has a view of the whole human condition and of our particular concern at the moment? Who has seen the whole script of our life experiences, and of this latest episode? Who can keep a lifetime of lessons in focus? Who can speak truth amidst the babble of opinions? For the person of faith, only God's wisdom answers all human needs.

"Worldly wisdom" is uncertain; people change their minds, and cultures change their values. What is "street smart" in one context may be supremely foolish in another time and place. God's wisdom never changes, and never needs to—the Creator's instructions for His Creation tell us how things really work, no matter how confusing human opinions may be.

According to Proverbs:

- 2:6 *For the Lord grants wisdom! His every word is a treasure of knowledge and understanding.*

"If you want to know what God wants you to do, ask him, and he will gladly tell you, for he is always ready to give a bountiful supply of wisdom to all who ask him... (James 1:5)." "For God gives those who please him wisdom, knowledge, and joy... (Ecclesiastes 2:26)." "Nothing is perfect except your words.... They make me wiser than my enemies.... Yes, wiser than my teachers.... Even wiser than the aged (Psalm 119:96-100)." "And wisdom and knowledge shall be the stability of thy times, and strength of salvation; the fear of the Lord is his treasure (Isaiah 33:6 KJV)." God guides His people as they seek and follow the wisdom of His Word.

- 3:4-6 *If you want favor with both God and man, and a reputation for good judgment and common sense, then trust the Lord completely; don't ever trust yourself. In everything you do, put God first, and He will direct you and crown your efforts with success.*

25

"When a man is trying to please God, God makes even his worst enemies to be at peace with him (Proverbs 16:7)." "Then said those men, We shall not find any occasion against this Daniel. Except we find it against him concerning the law of his God (Daniel 6:5 KJV)." "Oh, the joys of those who ... delight in doing everything God wants them to do, and day and night are always meditating on the his laws and thinking about ways to follow him more closely (Psalm 1:1, 2)." Pleasing God brings no offense to anyone—except those who find pleasing God offensive.

The fear of the Lord is not a religious mysticism which isolates a person from the challenges of life—it is a biblical realism which equips a person to meet those challenges. It is neither being too heavenly minded to be any earthly good, nor being too earthly minded to be any heavenly good. The fear of the Lord brings the wisdom of heaven into life on earth.

- 3:21 *Have two goals: wisdom-that is, knowing and doing right – and common sense.*
- 4:7 *Determination to be wise is the first step toward becoming wise! And with your wisdom, develop common sense and good judgment.*

"He [God] grants good sense to the godly-His saints. He is their shield, protecting them and guarding their pathway. He shows how to distinguish right from wrong, how to find the right decision every time (Proverbs 2:7-8)." "I, Wisdom, give good advice and common sense. Because of my strength, kings reign in power. I show the judges who is right and who is wrong. Rulers rule well with my help (Proverbs 8:15-16)." God's wisdom is both moral and practical—doing what is right will produce good results.

Wisdom must be a consciously chosen goal—learning by trial and error throughout a lifetime fills life with errors and trials. Everybody is a philosopher; we all have ways of thinking which color our view of the world. We need to test our vision by a more reliable standard, the standard of God's Word.

- 8:13 *If anyone respects and fears God, he will hate evil. For wisdom hates pride, arrogance, corruption and deceit of every kind.*

"Then the Lord asked Satan, 'Have you noticed my servant Job? He is the finest man in all the earth—a good man who fears God and will have nothing to do with evil (Job 1:8).'" "Stop loving this evil world and all that it offers you, for when you love these things you show that you do not really love God; for all these worldly things, these evil desires—the craze for sex, the ambition to buy everything that appeals to you, and the pride that comes from wealth and importance—these are not from God. They are from this evil world itself (I John 2:15-16)." "For jealousy and selfishness are not God's kind of wisdom. Such things are earthly, unspiritual, inspired by the devil (James 3:15)." God's people keep their distance from anything which dishonors God or is contrary to His character.

- 9:9-10 *Teach a wise man, and he will be the wiser; teach a good man, and he will learn more; For the reverence and fear of God are basic to all wisdom. Knowing God results in every other kind of understanding.*

"Show me the path where I should go, O Lord; point out the right road for me to walk. Lead me, teach me, for you are the God who gives me salvation. I have no hope except in you…. Where is the man who fears the Lord? God will teach him how to choose the best (Psalm 25:4-5, 12)." "A wise man will hear, and will increase learning; and a man of understanding shall attain unto wise counsels (Proverbs 1:5 KJV)." A teachable spirit characterizes those who seek God's wisdom—they are lifetime learners, not stagnant "know-it-alls."

Wisdom is directly related to action—our behavior reveals our real beliefs. God's wisdom is not abstract mental fluff; it is a way of thinking which produces a way of living. Our faith is our life. If what we say we believe about God does not affect how we do business, we are deceiving ourselves.

- 16:22 *Wisdom is a fountain of life to those possessing it, but a fool's burden is his folly.*

"The words of a man's mouth are like deep waters, and the wellspring of wisdom like a flowing brook…. A fool's mouth is his destruction, and his lips are the snare of his soul (Proverbs 18:4, 7 KJV)." "But the wisdom which comes from heaven is first of all pure and full of quiet gentleness. Then it is peace-loving and courteous. It allows discussion and is willing to yield to others; it is full of mercy and good deeds. It is wholehearted and straightforward and sincere (James 3:17)." God's wisdom is compassionate and calm; worldly wisdom is competitive and often contentious. And sometimes downright nasty, as was recently reported on many major news medias where several chicken producing plant supervisors were accused of exploiting their workers by not allowing them to have bathroom breaks. Workers in fear of losing their jobs by taking a bathroom break resorted to wearing adult diapers while processing chickens on the line. Whoever these supervisors were, whatever their motivations, they acted not only inhuman but very foolishly.

Abigail's Aid

Abigail's husband was Fool. Yes, really. That was his name—in Hebrew "Nabal" means, "fool." Somehow, this man had gotten rich, and enjoyed living in prosperity. He had three thousand sheep (I Samuel 25:2-3). Three thousand hungry sheep can cover quite a lot of territory, so Nabal's herdsmen ranged far and wide to keep them healthy. Considering that the area was hilly, with plenty of caves to hide in, the threats from enemy raiding parties and bands of outlaws kept people awake counting their sheep. Besides that, the king was subject to fits of rage, and often roamed the countryside with his army, chasing after an elusive harp-playing shepherd boy. A man with three thousand sheep should have appreciated any help he could get to protect his investment. But Nabal was a fool.

That harp-playing shepherd boy had grown up, and a bunch of misfits were running with him. Besides family members, everyone who was distressed, discontent, or in debt joined up. Given the condition of the country, it's surprising that there were only four hundred of them

(I Samuel 22:1-2). The grown-up shepherd boy had a few things going for him: he was tough enough to fight lions and giants and bears (Oh, my!), and God's prophet had already anointed him as God's choice to be the next king. The man's name was David, and he was no fool.

David and his men had to scrounge for food anywhere they could, and they tried to be nice about it. For example, they didn't make mutton stew out of Nabal's sheep. It would have been easy enough for four hundred men to pick off a few choice sheep. Who could stop them? And who would miss a few lamb chops out of a herd of three thousand? But David's gang didn't take even one sheep, and they saw to it that nobody else did, either. Nabal should have had them over for lunch, and least. But he was a fool.

When it came time to bring the sheep together for shearing, there would be something like a party. The shearing itself would be a flurry of activity, accompanied by celebration, and rewards for work well done. Although he had rendered valuable service, David did not receive an invitation. He RSVP'd, anyway, politely requesting whatever Nabal might choose to give him and his men. Nabal absolutely refused, calling David and his men rebellious nobodies, who would certainly come to no good end. Nabal was a mean-spirited fool.

Cutting to the chase—or rather, skipping the chase because David did not attack—Abigail intervened. She listened to the shepherds when they told her of David's help and Nabal's foolish reaction. On her own initiative, she packed lunch for four hundred, and headed out. She convinced David to spare Nabal (I Samuel 25:14-35).

Meanwhile, back at the party, Nabal was drinking himself silly. Actually, it was worse than that. The next morning when Abigail told him how close they had been to disaster, Nabal was stone cold sober. Really. "His heart died within him, and he became as a stone (I Samuel 25:37). He died ten days later. It's true what they say about a fool and his money.

• 19:8 *He who loves wisdom loves his own best interest and will be a success.*

"Oh, the joys of those who ... delight in doing what God wants them to ... They are like trees along a river bank bearing luscious fruit each season without fail. Their leaves shall not wither, and all they do shall prosper (Psalm 1:1-3)." "For I know the plans I have for you, says the Lord. They are plans for good and not for evil, to give you a future, and a hope (Jeremiah 29:11)." Following God's wisdom leads to true satisfaction.

Wisdom is what works, consistently and ultimately. Buying up all the latest self-help books of one decade only supplies recycled material (paper and placebos) for the self-help books of the next decade. Human wisdom shifts, sidesteps, and falls. Only God's wisdom is timeless.

• 21:22 *The wise man conquers the strong man and levels his defenses.*

• 24:5 *A wise man is mightier than a strong man.*
   Wisdom is mightier than strength.

"'Not by might, nor by power, but by my Spirit, says the Lord of Hosts—you will succeed because of my Spirit, though you are few and weak (Zechariah 4:6).'" "Some trust in chariots, and some in horses: but we will remember the name of the LORD our God (Psalm 20:7 KJV)." "The speed of a horse is nothing to him. How puny in his sight is the strength of a man. But his joy is in those who reverence him, those who expect him to be loving and kind (Psalm 147:10-11)." "I walk in the strength of the Lord God. I tell everyone that you alone are just and good (Psalm 71:16)." "But in that coming day, no weapon that is formed against you shall succeed ... This is the heritage of the servants of the Lord. This is the blessing I have given you, says the Lord (Isaiah 54:17)." The Word of God will accomplish God's purposes (Isaiah 55:11). When God's people are living according to God's wisdom as it is revealed in

God's Word, they, too, will accomplish every purpose God has for them.

"Work smarter, not harder" has been a slogan of efficiency experts. "A dull axe requires great strength; be wise and sharpen the blade (Ecclesiastes 10:10)." People who work with their hands know the value of having the right tools for the job, and the wisdom of keeping tools in excellent condition.

Our minds need to be maintained, too — cleansed of impurities, sharp, precise, and accurate. Most labor-saving devices show evidence that somebody who knew how to do a job the hard way was motivated to find a simpler way to do it. Wisdom not only improves efficiency, but also brings better results than brute force.

True wisdom is not abstract philosophical reasoning, but nuts-and-bolts common sense about the way things really work.

The Bible is not escapist literature — it speaks to the grittiest realities of life with the clear voice of the Creator and Redeemer of humankind. God is not aloof from our struggles; He is with us in the midst of our most perplexing and demanding circumstances, ready to give us wisdom to go on in the right direction. The knowledge that the living God is present and active in our lives gives us strong reason to commit ourselves to His care and guidance.

Conviction defines Character

The fear of the Lord is not blind terror of unknown supernatural forces — it is reasonable respect for the living God. The fear of the Lord is not just a religious feeling — it is a commitment to seek and follow the wisdom of the God of the Bible. The fear of the Lord means laying aside mere worldly wisdom and accepting what God says as authoritative for every aspect of our lives.

"But, my son be warned: there is no end of opinions ready to be expressed. Studying them can go on forever, and become very exhausting! Here is my final conclusion: fear God and obey his commandments, for this is the entire duty of man. For God will judge us for everything we do, including every hidden thing, good or bad (Ecclesiastes 12:13-14)."

What we believe makes us who we are. Our perceptions of ourselves, and our patterns of interaction with others, are based in our fundamental assumptions about reality. If God
is the center of reality, our thought, speech, and action will demonstrate our obedient faith in Him. If we make ourselves the center of reality, and everybody else is just as self-centered, life becomes a ruthless competition.

Caleb's Claim

Caleb was "the other good spy"—Joshua got the promotion, and wrote the book, but Caleb was right there with him on the reconnaissance mission into the Promised Land. Joshua and Caleb saw the God of the
promise, and wanted to claim everything God had for them. The other ten spies saw the problems of the land, and opted for Plan B. The people accepted the majority report, and nearly executed Joshua and Caleb for their audacity. After muddling around for forty years waiting for the nay-sayers to die off, Joshua was ready to lead a new generation into the land. Caleb had not dropped out of the picture, but clung to a snapshot he had taken on their spy mission. He had seen the giants, the enemy armies, and the fortified cities which stirred paralyzing fear in his fellow spies. But he had also seen a glorious mountain, the place of God's specific promise to him. He never lost sight of that mountain through all the dusty wanderings in the wilderness. The prospect of claiming God's promise stirred energizing faith within Caleb's heart.

Forty years earlier, Caleb had been sure that God would empower His people to take possession of everything He wanted them to have. His vision had not been blurred by the trials of the road. Now they were entering the land. The giants, the armies, and the fortifications were still there. But Caleb was still walking with God, and had not lost sight of the promise. The man who had urged the people to "go up at once" to possess their possessions, now said, "Give me this mountain (Numbers 13:30; Joshua 14:12)."

Still walking with God, Caleb claimed his mountain. It took more work than might have been expected of a man in his eighties, but he was walking with God, and "superhuman effort" was readily available. Interestingly, Caleb's claim did not result in selfishly hoarded prosperity. He gave his daughter in marriage to a man who helped secure the claim, and gave her the double inheritance she requested (Joshua 15:16-19). Hebron, at the center of Caleb's claim, was set apart as a city of the Levites (Joshua 21:9-12).What sense does this make?

Walking with God, we see life through the eyes of faith. Early on, we may get a clear view of what God can do in and through us. There may be many obstacles and little human encouragement, but we never lose sight of the promise. In fact, life becomes a quest to become everything God wants to make us, and to do all the good works He has planned for us. Our heart's cry is, "Give me this mountain!"

Yet, as we claim our possessions, we find that they are to be used to bless others and to worship God.

May Caleb's claim be our example as we lay hold of God's promises and devote our lives to seeing their fulfillment.

Character

Who we are determines what we do.

Who are we? We are people who are called to conform to the image of Christ, people who are God's representatives on earth. Conformity to Christ (Romans 8:29; Ephesians 4:13) and the fruit of the Spirit (Galatians 5:22-23) will make us people of integrity. As Christ is "formed in us" (Galatians 4:19), His image will be reflected in our approach to our work and to the people who work with us. In our financial and business relationships, that means we are people who can be trusted, and people who can trust others. Within ourselves, we are to be honest, loving, and loyal persons. In relation to others, we are to be teachable, considerate, and humble.

We speak more about characters than about character. We quote and imitate favorite characters from movies and books. Even cartoon characters leave lasting impressions. There's a reason for that. Film-makers, authors, and animators want to create personalities which catch our attention. They want to make an impression.

The impression a character leaves is, in fact, "character." In Hebrews 1:3, the Greek word which may be transliterated, "character," is commonly translated, "express image." Jesus is the "express image," or character, of God's person. An express image was an exact copy made by stamping or engraving—a permanent accurate representation.

That's what we should be talking about when we talk about character. How well do we represent the ideals we profess? Do statements of our business ethics match the way we actually do business? Have we been pressed into the world's mold, coming out as copies of some successful entrepreneur? Or does our character bear the stamp of the character of Jesus Christ—the very character of God?

Character within ourselves

Character grows from conviction. Our beliefs about what constitutes reality affect our thoughts, emotions, and choices. A worldview becomes a mindset. The godly wisdom which comes from a fear of the Lord calms God's people. As we absorb God's Word, we begin to stand where God stands, and to see what God sees. Thinking what God thinks makes a person say what God says, and act like God acts. Saying what God says, in fact, is the essence of our confession of faith, and our confession of sins — even in Greek, the word translated "confession" means "same-saying." It all begins internally, as the Holy Spirit uses the Word of God to transform our minds. Character comes from deep inside, where our most fundamental assumptions about reality form the roots of everything we think, feel, and choose.

Honesty

Better Heaven with empty pockets than Hell with pockets full. Integrity is always the best policy. Here are some facts I hope you won't lose sight of: In life you reap what you sow (Galatians 6:7); sow to the wind, and reap a whirlwind (Hosea 8:7). Make sure you are right before you go ahead. Remember that "some men...lead sinful lives and everyone knows it...in other cases only the judgment day will reveal the terrible truth (I Timothy 5:24)." It is appointed unto man once to die and then the judgment (Hebrews 9:27 KJV)." Our accountability to God is of even higher importance than our success and our reputation among men. Those who choose the higher road of "honesty is the best policy," and always do what they say, will have loyal customers and repeat business. Most importantly, your business will be favored by the Lord. Truthfulness is essential to the character of God (Romans 3:4). Jesus is "the truth (John 14:6)." The fruit of the Holy Spirit is "goodness, righteousness, and truth (Ephesians 5:9). If the character of God, as revealed in Christ, is being worked into our lives, our character will epitomize transparent honesty.

According to Proverbs:

• 11:1 *The Lord hates cheating and delights in honesty.*

"Though everyone else in the world is a liar, God is not (Romans 3:4)." Jesus told Pilate, "I came to bring truth to the world. All who love the truth are my followers (John 18:37)." No matter how common deception is in accepted business practice, it has no place in the character or conduct of a child of God. In fact, deceitfulness is characteristic of children of the devil: "You are children of your father the devil, and you love to do the evil things he does ... When he lies, it is perfectly normal; for he is the father of liars (John 8:44)."

• 12:14 *Telling the truth gives a man great satisfaction, and hard work returns many blessings to him.*

After a lifetime of public service, Samuel challenged the people of Israel to cite any instance of theft, fraud, oppression, or bribery during his ministry. "'No,' they replied, 'you have never defrauded or oppressed us in any way and you have never taken even one single bribe' (I Samuel 12:4)." Insider trading, pay-to-play politics, and Ponzi schemes bring eventual exposure and disgrace; honesty in business brings peace and contentment.

Honesty reflects God's character and brings peace and contentment. Honest people sleep better; they are not troubled by guilt or fear of exposure. As has been truly said, liars have to have very good memories—only the truth comes out exactly the same every time it is said.

• 22:1 *If you must choose, take a good name rather than great riches; for to be held in loving esteem is better than silver and gold.*

Seeking riches at the expense of relationships leads to loneliness, dishonor, and judgment. James warns those who oppress others for material gain, "Look here, you rich men, now is the time to cry and groan with anguished grief

because of all the terrible troubles ahead of you (James 5:1)."
Building relationships through good character brings honor and
contentment: "For the good man—the blameless, the upright,
the man of peace—he has a wonderful future ahead of him. For
him there is a happy ending.

- 11:3a *A good man is guided by his honesty.*
- 11:5a *The upright are directed by their honesty.*

"Do things in such a way that everyone can see you
are honest clear through (Romans 12:17). Followers of Christ
are to demonstrate His character to the world: "You are to live
clean, innocent lives as children of God in a dark world full of
people who are crooked and stubborn. Shine out among them
like beacon lights (Philippians 2:15)." Paul set an example of
accountability in handling donations for ministry; "By traveling
together we will guard against any suspicion, for we are anxious
that no one should find fault with the way we are handling this
large gift. God knows we are honest, but I want everyone else
to know it, too. That is why we have made this arrangement
(II Corinthians 8:20-21)."

Honesty assures both self-respect and the respect of
others. If we are transparent ourselves, we will see through the
false fronts dishonest people put up. Honesty means that every
person we have dealt with, and every word we have spoken, will
only confirm our integrity. A man for all seasons is a man whose
character endures through every contingency of life.

- 11:4 *Your riches won't help you on Judgment Day; only*
  righteousness counts then.

"They trust in their wealth and boast about how rich
they are, yet not one of them, though rich as kings, can ransom
his own brother from the penalty of sin! For God's forgiveness
does not come that way. For a soul is far too precious to be
ransomed by mere earthly wealth. There is not enough of it in all
the earth to buy eternal life for just one soul, to keep it out of hell
(Psalm 49:6-9)."

• 20:7   *It is a wonderful heritage to have an honest father.*

"Blessing on all who reverence and trust the Lord—on all who obey him…. Your wife shall be contented in your home. And look at all those children! They sit around the table as vigorous and healthy as olive trees (Psalm 128:1, 3)." Those who fear the Lord are committed to living "a quiet and peaceable life in all godliness and honesty (I Timothy 2:2 KJV)." The result is a stable family life in which children thrive.

Honesty has value for both time and eternity. God has established the rules of the game of life—cheaters lose. It is a horrible embarrassment for surviving family members to discover that the "dearly departed" was secretly a liar, a thief, and a scoundrel. For the dearly departed, there is infinitely greater dismay at facing the judgment of God. Displaying God's character in their lives, God's people have no fear of condemnation, and their families are blessed by their example and their memory.

• 16:11   *The Lord demands fairness in every business deal. He*
           established this principle.

"Use accurate measurements—lengths, weights, and volumes—and give full measure, for I am Jehovah your God … (Leviticus 19:36)." "You must use honest scales, honest bushels, honest gallons (Ezekiel 45:10)." "God's people are to use no "tricks of the trade" to gain an advantage over clients or customers.

• 20:23   *The Lord loathes all cheating and dishonesty.*

• 20:10   *The Lord despises every kind of cheating.*

"All who cheat with unjust weights and measurements are detestable to the Lord your God (Deuteronomy 25:13)." "'Utterly worthless!' says the buyer as he haggles over the price. But afterwards he brags about his bargain (Proverbs 20:14)." Whether selling or buying, the child of God will place fair value on goods or services.

Truthfulness should be essential to our approach to all business matters. "Honesty is the best policy" is not enough. We are not honest because that is what works to our advantage—we are honest because that is the very character of God in us, and because it is what pleases Him

- 28:6   *Better to be poor and honest than rich and a cheater.*
- 16:8   *A little gained honestly, is better than great wealth gotten by dishonest means.*

"It is better to have little and be godly than to own an evil man's wealth; for the strength of evil men shall be broken, but the Lord takes care of those he has forgiven (Psalm 37:16-17)." "But people who long to be rich soon begin to do all kinds of wrong things to get money, things that hurt them and make them evil-minded and finally send them to hell itself (I Timothy 6:9)." "The man who works hard sleeps well whether he eats little or much, but the rich must worry and suffer insomnia (Ecclesiastes 5:12)." Honest work for honest gain brings peace and contentment; dishonest greed brings fear and ultimate disaster.

Dishonesty is often excused as "shrewd dealing," making quick gains by slick means. But 'what goes around comes around," and shrewd dealers eventually reap what they sow.

According to Proverbs:

- 21:6   *Dishonest gain will never last, so why take the risk?*

"Like a bird that fills her nest with young she has not hatched and which will soon desert her and fly away, so is the man who gets his wealth by unjust means. Sooner or later he will lose his riches and at the end of his life become a poor old fool (Jeremiah 17:11)." Many people who have gained wealth "hand over fist" by manipulating other people's money have seen their gains slip through their fingers just as rapidly.

- 10:2   *Ill-gotten gains bring no lasting happiness; right living does.*

"What a slippery path they are on — suddenly God will send them sliding over the edge of the cliff and down to their destruction: an instant end to all their happiness, an eternity of terror (Psalm 73:18-19)." Money can buy temporary pleasure, comfort, and diversion; true happiness is found only in knowing and serving God. "You will keep on guiding me all my life with your wisdom and counsel; and afterwards receive me into the glories of heaven (Psalm 73:24)."

Even P.T. Barnum, the great showman, knew that it is impossible to fool all of the people all of the time. "Some men's sins are open beforehand, going before to judgment; and some men they follow after (I Timothy 5:24 KJV)." "... you may be sure that your sin will catch up with you (Numbers 32:23)," Fraud is eventually exposed — any gain gotten deceitfully is precarious, at best.

- 20:17 *Some men enjoy cheating, but the cake they buy with such ill-gotten gain will turn to gravel in their mouths.*
- 20:21 *A fortune can be made from cheating, but there is a curse that goes with it.*
- 5:27a *Dishonest money brings grief to all the family.*

"Don't you realize that ever since man was first placed on earth, the triumph of the wicked has been short-lived, and the joy of the godless but for a moment? His labors will not be rewarded; wealth will give him no joy (Job 20:4, 18)." "Let everyone be sure he is doing his very best, for then he will have the personal satisfaction of work well done... (Galatians 6:4)." "Do you want to be truly rich? You already are if you are happy and good (I Timothy 6:6)." The pleasures ill-gotten money can buy are fleeting — lasting contentment comes from honest, productive work.

- 28:18 *Good men will be rescued from harm, but cheaters will be destroyed.*

"Although the wicked flourish like weeds, there is only eternal destruction ahead of them.... But the Godly shall flourish like palm trees, and grow tall as the cedars of Lebanon. For they are transplanted into the Lord's own garden, and are under his personal care (Psalm 93:7, 12)." Those who gain wealth deceitfully will fall just as quickly as they rise—just like fast-growing short-lived weeds. Those who follow God's wisdom grow slowly and securely—like firmly rooted trees. God judges the wicked, but carefully tends to the needs of his own people, to make them productive and contented.

Fraud carries the seeds of its own destruction. When deceitfulness becomes engrained in one's character, suspicion and fear take control of one's life. What if everyone is as dishonest as I am? Can I trust anybody? Ultimately, there are no secrets—a web of lies will soon entangle the one who fabricates it. Duplicity brings it's owner disgrace. Double-dealing is the work of a madman in business and in life. Arrogance is where fools abide. Honest people enjoy God's blessing as well as the respect and goodwill of the people around them.

Love   If you love those who work for you, they will know it. The working conditions will be well-suited to health and safety; their future will be secure; efforts rewarded and suggestions heeded; and comfort and welfare will be anticipated. The only way to defeat hate is to love deeply. "Love covers a multitude of sins"; the only way to overcome great sin is to love a lot. "Love your enemies," said the Master. How much more your friends and associates? Working conditions are much more important than money alone. Many well-paid sales people work for less money than they could make somewhere else because they are valued and respected. The story of Dataflex by President and C.E.O. Rick Rose, *How to Make A Buck and Still Be a Nice Guy*, illustrates the point. Rick treated his sales people so well that they loved to work for him. He always has top sales people who could have taken their pick of any Fortune Five Hundred company, but remained with Rick because of his abilities to motivate, praise and capture their very best for the company.

Love is essential to the character of God (John 3:16). "God is love (I John 4:8)." Jesus commanded His followers to love one another as He loved them (John 13:34-35). If the character of God, as revealed in Christ, is being worked into our lives, our character will epitomize unconditional love.

According to Proverbs:

- 8:21 *Those who love and follow me are indeed wealthy. I fill their treasuries.*

"Trust in the LORD, and do good; so shalt thou dwell in the land, and verily thou shalt be fed (Psalm 37:3 KJV)." "And if you will carefully obey all of his commandments... and if you will love the Lord your God with all your hearts and souls, and will worship him, then he will continue to send both the early and late rains that will produce wonderful crops of grain, grapes for your wine, and olive oil. He will give you lush pastureland for your cattle to graze in, and you yourselves shall have plenty to eat and be fully content (Deuteronomy 11:13-15)." Loving God is not a mere religious sensitivity—it is a lifelong commitment to conform to God's revealed will. Communion with God in spiritual life is expressed as obedience to God in material life. On His part, God commits Himself to sustain His people both spiritually and materially.

- 4:11 *I would have you learn this great fact: that a life of doing right is the wisest life there is.*

"...He has told you what he wants, and this is all it is: to be fair and just and merciful, and to walk humbly with your God (Micah 6:8)." A life of obedient faith works God's character into our own character. Since this is God's purpose for us, it is the only way to live truly successfully (Romans 8:28-29)."

Love should be essential to our approach to all business matters. We should quit worrying about the rat-race and show more concern for the human race. Money cannot buy God's favor, and financial success is not the true measure of a person's value in God's sight.

According to Proverbs:

- 22:2 *The rich and the poor are alike before the Lord who made them all.*

"How can you claim that you belong to the Lord Jesus Christ, the Lord of glory, if you show favoritism to rich people and look down on poor people (James 2:1)." "For he doesn't care how great a man may be, and doesn't pay any more attention to the rich than to the poor. He made them all (Job 34:19)." "Some he causes to be poor and others to be rich... (I Samuel 2:7)." We may be tempted to prefer materially successful people because we think they must be wiser or more spiritual than less wealthy people. But, "God has chosen poor people to be rich in faith... (James 2:5)." Obedient faith is demonstrated by contentment and unconditional love.

- 29:7 *The good man knows the poor man's rights; the godless don't care.*

"Give fair judgment to the poor man, the afflicted, the fatherless, the destitute. Rescue the poor and needy from the grasp of evil men (Psalm 82:3-4)." "Anyone who oppresses the poor is insulting God who made them. To help the poor is to honor God (Proverbs 14:31)." "If I have been unfair to my servants, how could I face God? What could I say when he questioned me about it? For God made me, and made my servant too. He created us both (Job 31:13-15)." "Judges must always be just in their sentences, not noticing whether a person is poor or rich: they must always be perfectly fair (Leviticus 19:15)." Those in positions of authority in business or in government tend to be most comfortable with "their own kind"—people of similar social and financial standing. God sees only humankind.

Those who value money more than people become extremely class-conscious. Obsessed with their own grasping for riches, they treat those who are content with less as somewhat less human. "Enjoy prosperity whenever you can, and when hard times strike, realize that God gives one as well as the

43

other—so that everyone will realize that nothing is certain in this life (Ecclesiastes 7:14." "For who maketh thee to differ from another? and what hast thou that thou didst not receive? now if thou didst receive it, why dost thou glory, as if thou hadst not received it? (I Corinthians 4:7)." God does not recognize artificial barriers people build—His grace and His judgment make no socio-economic distinctions.

• 21:15 *A good man loves justice, but it is calamity to evildoers*

"Praise the Lord! For all who fear God and trust in him are blessed beyond expression. Yes, happy is the man who delights in doing his commands ... He is kind and merciful—and all goes well for the generous man who conducts his business fairly ... Evil-minded men will be infuriated when they see all this; they will gnash their teeth in anger and slink away, their hopes thwarted (Psalm 112:1, 4-5, 10)." Those whose character conforms to God's character enjoy the benefits of his justice—those who are characterized by deceitful shrewdness suffer the consequences of God's judgment.

• 12:22 *God loves those who keep their promises and hates those who don't.*

"The Lord has commanded that when anyone makes a promise to the Lord, either to do something or to quit doing something, that vow must not be broken: the person making the vow must do exactly as he has promised (Numbers 30:1-2)." "When you make a vow to the Lord, be prompt in doing whatever it is you promised him, for the Lord demands that you promptly fulfill your vows: it is a sin if you don't (Deuteronomy 23:21)." "Lord, who may go and find refuge and shelter in your tabernacle and your holy hill? Anyone who leads a blameless life and is truly sincere… keeps a promise even if it ruins him (Psalm 15:1, 6)." God keeps His promises—those who reflect His character keep theirs.

Love can be tough, giving and receiving constructive criticism. Hatred is based on fear of personal loss or injury—

love casts out that fear (I John 4:18). Love brings calm confidence even in times of stress. Lasting conflict resolution is won by those who maintain mutual respect and civility while dealing candidly with differences.

- 19:8 *He who loves wisdom loves his own best interest and will be a success*

"And wisdom and knowledge shall be the stability of thy times, and strength of salvation: the fear of the LORD is his treasure (Isaiah 33:6 KJV)." Obedient faith brings wisdom which stabilizes and strengthens a person in all circumstances.

- 9:8b *... a wise man, when rebuked, will love you all the more*

"It is a badge of honor to accept valid criticism (Proverbs 25:12)." "Wounds from a friend are better than kisses from an enemy! (Proverbs 27:6)." "In the end, people appreciate frankness more than flattery (Proverbs 28:23)." "It is better to be criticized by a wise man than to be praised by a fool (Ecclesiastes 7:5)." Wise people, no matter how successful, will not believe their own "hype"—they will welcome and profit from constructive criticism. An honest critic among a horde of yes-men will be well-appreciated by the wise.

- 27:5 *Open rebuke is better than hidden love!*

"Don't hate your brother. Rebuke anyone who sins; don't let him get away with it, or you will be equally guilty (Leviticus 19:17)." God disciplines the ones He loves (Hebrews 12:6). Refusing to warn a sinner is not indifference, but hatred—not caring about the ultimate consequences of his or her sin. "I love them too much to say anything" is an unbiblical excuse, meaning simply, "I don't want to jeopardize a shallow relationship." Love is never silent when a loved one is in danger of great harm, even if self-inflicted.

In the old story, the Emperor did not know he had no clothes because nobody dared to tell him the truth. He was deluded by his own pride as well as by his tailor's deceit. "Pride goes before destruction and haughtiness before a fall (Proverbs

16:18)." An "accountability group" of like-minded yes-men will never correct a leader's self-delusion. True friends correct each other's vision by bringing productive insight to each other's blind spots.

• 20:3 *It is an honor for a man to stay out of a fight.*

"Yanking a dog's ears is no more foolish than interfering in an argument that isn't any of your business (Proverbs 26:17)." "And those who are peacemakers will plant seeds of peace and reap a harvest of goodness (James 3:18)." When emotions run high, understanding runs low—contentious people just want to vent their opinions (Proverbs 18:1-2). It is better to avoid the heat of the argument, and to seek peace through calm, patient discussion at a more appropriate time.

• 10:12 *Hatred stirs old quarrels, but love overlooks insults.*

• 17:9a *Love forgets mistakes.*

"It [love] is not irritable or touchy. It does not hold grudges and will hardly even notice when others do it wrong (I Corinthians 13:5)." "Stop being mean, bad-tempered and angry. Quarreling, harsh words, and dislike of others should have no place in your lives (Ephesians 4:31)." "Most important of all, continue to show deep love for each other, for love makes up for many of your faults (I Peter 4:8)." Dwelling on offenses and disagreements is counter-productive, paralyzing relationships and poisoning one's heart and mind. Healthy relationships and productive cooperation grow as love builds on areas of agreement and mutual encouragement.

"Looking out for Number One" tends to alienate everybody else. The person whose motto is "I know my rights!" often runs roughshod over everybody else's rights. "You've got to stick up for yourself—nobody else will!!" Oh, really? "If God be for us, who can be against us (Romans 8:31 KJV)?" We can present evidence and use persuasion to defend ourselves when attacked, but it is counterproductive to pick fights and hold grudges—especially when God Himself is looking out for our best interests.

"God is love, and anyone who lives in love is living with God and God is living in him (I John 4:16)." Love is at the core of God's character, and at the core of the character of His true followers. God's love is not mere emotion, but a settled attitude of security in one's own person, and of openness to the needs of others. The New Testament reveals the love of God in its fullness in Jesus Christ, and includes many calls for us to experience and express that love (I Corinthians 13 most notably).

Loyalty

Some company managers and business owners complain that they can't find staff who are faithful. It is true that loyalty can't be bought at any price. True loyalty is a result of mutual respect and admiration. We can and should learn something from almost everyone; "even a fool teaches us what not to do" (also see Proverbs 21:11-12).

But loyalty is more than learning. Loyalty involves investing in another and seeing it through. In your business, invest in those who work for you, treating them the way you would like to be treated in the same job or situation.

My colleague and friend Ed Wheat, M.D., always let his office staff off for lunch, or for the day, anytime their mates were off. The result: a staff which was faithful and appreciative with many years of service. The workplace was encouraging, rewarding, fair, and fun. In fourteen years of daily work I never heard even one word of complaint or saw an ounce of anger; only positive words of praise, encouragement, and appreciation. Imitate Dr. Wheat's methods, and you won't have to worry about good help; they will find you.

Faithfulness is essential to the character of God (Deuteronomy 7:9; Lamentations 3:23). Jesus is the same, "yesterday, today, and forever (Hebrews 13:8)." We can lay aside greed, trusting the Lord Who will never leave or forsake us (Hebrews 13:5). If the character of God, as revealed in Christ, is being worked into our lives, our character will epitomize unchanging faithfulness.

According to Proverbs:

• 17:17a *A true friend is always loyal.*

"…David met Jonathan, the king's son, and there was an immediate bond of love between them…. Jonathan swore to be his blood brother I Samuel 18:1, 3)." "Prince Jonathan now went to find David… and encouraged him in his faith in God (I Samuel 23:16)." "And David said, 'Is there yet any that is left of the house of Saul, that I may show him kindness for Jonathan's sake (II Samuel 9:1 KJV)?'" Even at the risk of his own right to the throne, Jonathan protected and encouraged his friend David. When David became king, he wanted to protect and encourage members of Saul's family out of loyalty to his friend Jonathan. True friendship is grounded in unchanging mutual respect and affection, not in changing circumstances.

• 27:10a *Never abandon a friend …*

"My best friends abhor me. Those I loved have turned against me (Job 19:19)." "My loved ones and friends stay away, fearing my disease. Even my own family stands at a distance (Psalm 38:11)." "… For God has said, 'I will never, never fail you nor forsake you (Hebrews 13:5).'" Without loyal friends, life's troubles wound us more deeply—without encouragement, we fall into discouragement and despair. God's character includes unvarying faithfulness. Those who bear His name should show similar loyalty to those who rely on them.

Loyalty is sometimes simply "being there" for a friend. Job's friends came to his side in his time of greatest need. Sitting silently with him, their presence assured him that he was not alone. When they opened their mouths, they became "miserable comforters"—their judgmental comments did not do justice to Job, and their theology was too shallow (Job 16:2; 42:7)." A true friend comes alongside to strengthen our faith, not to feed our fears.

- 18:24 *Some people are friends in name only. Others are closer than brothers.*
- 20:6 *Most people will tell you what loyal friends they are, but are they telling the truth?*

"A wealthy man has many 'friends'; the poor man has none left (Proverbs 19:4)." "Even his own neighbors despise the poor man, while the rich have many 'friends' (Proverbs 14:20)." People like to be associated with worldly success. Wealth attracts; poverty repels. The wealthy have many fair-weather friends who will abandon them when reversals come. Many people will associate with you in good times—a true friend compassionately shares all of the ups and downs of life.

Success of any kind attracts hangers-on, people who hope to gain something through association with the successful. Always name-dropping and networking, they lose the capacity for relationships based on trust and affection—they are constantly looking for "angles," ways to get some selfish advantage from every acquaintance.

- 25:13 *A faithful employee is as refreshing as a cool day in the hot summer time.*

"Now the most important thing about a servant is that he does just what his master tells him to (I Corinthians 4:2)." "Slaves, obey your masters; be eager to give them your very best. Serve them as you would Christ. Don't work hard only when your master is watching you and then shirk when he isn't looking; work hard and with gladness all the time, as though working for Christ, doing the will of God with all your hearts (Ephesians 6:5-7." "So Potiphar gave Joseph the complete administrative responsibility over everything he owned. He hadn't a worry in the world with Joseph there ..." "... The jailer soon handed over the entire prison administration to Joseph ... (Genesis 39:6, 32)." "Then the king made Daniel very great;

he gave him many costly gifts, and appointed him to be ruler over the whole province of Babylon, as well as chief over all his wise men (Daniel 2:48)." Faith in God builds faithfulness in all relationships and responsibilities. Joseph and Daniel both exemplify how God's people live out God's character even in the most adverse situations.

• 26:10 *The master may get better work from an untrained apprentice than from a skilled rebel.*

"You slaves must always obey your earthly masters, not only trying to please them when they are watching you but all the time; obey them willingly because of your love for the Lord and because you want to please him. Work hard and cheerfully at all you do, just as though you were working for the Lord and not merely for your masters, remembering that it is the Lord Christ who is going to pay you, giving you your full portion of all he owns. He is the one you are really working for (Colossians 3:22-24)."

A rebellious employee works against the best interest of an employer, doing less than the best possible job, or even sabotaging projects. God's people work for God's purposes, even in their earthly jobs. If you cannot imagine God hiring a person to do what you do. It may be time to look for a different career.

As someone long ago said, ability is not as important as reliability. Skills and information can be learned; loyalty is a matter of character. A skillful employee may have selfish motives which sabotage his or her employer's interests. At whatever level, a person who respects and shares his employer's goals, and works consistently to meet them, is highly valued.

Mephibosheth's Meal Ticket

Even when reading a sentence about Mephibosheth, his name makes us slow down or stumble. When he was five years old, his father and grandfather—Jonathan and King Saul—were killed in battle, and his nurse grabbed him up and ran. She didn't slow down, so she did stumble. Mephibosheth fell. His injuries made him lame for the rest of his life. This presented real problems in the culture of his time. When strength in hand-to-hand combat is required of heroes, a physical handicap is looked down upon as a disqualifying weakness (II Samuel 5:6-8). A lame priest could not offer sacrifices, and an lame animal could not be offered as a sacrifice (Leviticus 21:18, Deuteronomy 15:21).

Mephibosheth had another strike against him—he was a member of a deposed royal family. Although family members tried to keep the throne after the Philistines killed Saul, they faced the continued opposition of forces following David. God had chosen David to be the next king, and David had won the hearts of the people through his victories over their enemies. David prevailed, and the house of Saul ended with the assassination of Mephibosheth's uncle, Ishbosheth (II Samuel 4:5).

Saul had sought to exterminate David for many years, so it would have been understandable if David had followed a custom of the times, and sought to exterminate Saul's descendents. But David was a man of character—in fact, "a man after [God's] own heart (I Samuel 13:14 KJV)." He would not seek personal revenge, because he believed that God chose him to be king, just as God had chosen Saul.

Besides that, David had made a vow of friendship with Jonathan, Saul's son and Mephibosheth's father. He agreed that he would be kind to Jonathan's descendents even after Jonathan's death (I Samuel 18:3; 20:13-17).

When David's kingdom settled into relative peace, David remembered his vow to Jonathan, and called for a search for any of Saul's descendents. When Mephibosheth was brought in, he was understandably terrified that David might execute him. David explained that he wanted to fulfill his vow of kindness out of loyalty to Jonathan. He restored Saul's land to Mephibosheth, and invited him to live at the palace, and to eat his meals with David, as one of his own sons (II Samuel 9).

The character of God's people reflects the character of God. Just as David brought a crippled exile to a place of honor at the king's table, God brings sinful rebels into His own banquet hall. Just as David remembered and kept his vow, God is true to His promises. If we are to be true ambassadors for Christ, true representatives of God in the world, we must be honest, compassionate, and loyal in all our relationships.

Character In Relation to Others

Character within ourselves establishes consistency in our relations to others. Integrity is a wholeness of character, a unity at the core of one's being. Character is revealed in relationships. We can have all kinds of illusions about ourselves, but what's really inside us comes out in our interaction with other people. As Charlie Brown said, "I love mankind; it's people I can't stand." Our fondest images of ourselves may be far different from what others see in us. Integrity, wholeness and oneness of character, means being the same person at all times, in all situations, and to all people.

Being consistent in relation to others displays godly character. Godly wisdom is patient and benevolent, willing to wait for an outcome that benefits everyone concerned. The fear of the Lord drives out fear of anybody else, making it unnecessary to be defensive about our interests, and willing to give others credit for productive ideas.

Believers are called to be "swift to hear" and "slow to speak" (James 1:19). In business, patient consideration of the opinions and needs of others builds a solid base of support among those who work with us. Only a fool is so un-teachable that he values only his own opinions (Proverbs 18:2).

Intelligence and Wisdom

Being closed-minded never accomplished anything but increased ignorance, and being angry leads to failure-whether it be in sports, marriage, or business. Sir Henry Taylor said:

"In the affairs of life or of business, it is not intellect that tells so much as heart, not genius so much as self-control, patience and discipline, regulated by judgment. Hence there is no better provision for the uses of either private or public life, than a fair share of ordinary good sense guided by rectitude, disciplined by experience and inspired by goodness, issued in practical wisdom. To an extent, goodness implies wisdom, the highest wisdom the union of the worldly with the spiritual, the correspondence of wisdom and goodness."

Most buy when everyone else is buying and sell when everyone else is selling, or all would be wealthy. The time to "invest" in generators was after Y2K, not before! Look at what is happening in the world and evaluate where the needs of a society will be. Graciously and artfully meet those needs in a Christ-honoring way, and you will always be in demand.

Wisdom is essential to the character of God (I Samuel 2:3; Job 9:4). Jesus is the wisdom of God (I Corinthians 1:24, 30). If the character of God, as revealed in Christ, is being worked into our lives, our character will epitomize wisdom.

According to Proverbs:

• 18:15: *The intelligent man is always open to new ideas. In fact, he looks for them.*

"Dear brothers, don't ever forget that it is best to listen much, speak little, and not become angry ... (James 1:9)." ""A wise man is hungry for truth, while the mocker feeds on trash (Proverbs 15:14)." "Get the facts at any price, and hold on tightly to all the good sense you can get (Proverbs 23:23)." It is amazing what you can learn if you pay attention to everybody.. It may be comfortable to consult only a close circle of sympathetic counselors, but sometimes the most productive insight comes from an unexpected source. Stifling fresh opinions or getting defensive about dissent will limit creativity and productivity.

• 19:11: *A wise man restrains his anger and overlooks insults. This is to his credit.*

"A short-tempered man is a fool. He hates the man who is patient (Proverbs 14:17)." "Keep away from angry, short-tempered men, lest you learn to be like them and endanger your soul (Proverbs 22:24)." "A hot-tempered man starts fights and gets into all kinds of trouble (Proverbs 29:22)." "The selfish man quarrels against every sound principle of conduct by demanding his own way. A rebel doesn't care about the facts. All he wants to do is yell (Proverbs 18:1-2)." "The man of few words and settled mind is wise; therefore, even a fool is thought to be wise when he is silent. It pays s him to keep his mouth shut (Proverbs 17:27-28)." Unrestrained anger is foolishly unproductive. Strong emotion is not sinful in itself, and can even be useful in motivating us to positive action. But unnecessary arguments and offenses can be avoided by wise self-control. In fact, the advantage in most conflicts goes to the one who remains calm. Quietly answering challenges and diverting attacks almost always moves people towards resolution of their disagreements.

When you're right, you can afford to be patient—if you aren't sure that you are right, you can't afford to be impatient. Wisdom sorts out ideas, including unwelcome ones, and accepts the most reasonable proposals—from whatever source. Wisdom even extracts positive ideas from negative opinions. The kernel of truth in criticism or insult can grow into the solution of an otherwise unforeseen problem.

• 3:21-26 *Have two goals: wisdom—that is knowing and doing right— and common sense. Don't let them slip away, for they fill you with living energy, and are a feather in your cap. They keep you safe from defeat and disaster and from stumbling off the trail. With them on guard you can sleep without fear; and you need not be afraid of disaster or the plots of wicked men: for the Lord is with you; He protects you.*

"Do you want to be truly rich? You already are if you are happy and good (I Timothy 6:6)." "But godliness with contentment is great gain (I Timothy 6:6 KJV)." Money cannot buy wisdom. News stories about celebrities have given definitive proof that money cannot buy common sense. Yet living wisely and sensibly is the only way to find true happiness. Living right is ultimately more satisfying than "living large," indulging in every extravagance possible. The security and stability of a life lived under God's guidance are to be treasured above material wealth. The Lord helps those who admit their need for His help—those who "help themselves" to every earthly pleasure or treasure are on their own.

- 3:13-15 *The man who knows right from wrong and has good judgment and common sense is happier than the man who is immensely rich! For such wisdom is far more valuable than precious jewels. Nothing else compares with it.*

"Give me an understanding mind so that I can govern your people well and know the difference between what is right and what is wrong... (I Kings 3:9)." "You will never be able to eat solid spiritual food and understand the deeper things of God's Word until you become better Christians and learn right from wrong by practicing doing right (Hebrews 5:14)." God will give His people wisdom to act ethically, fairly, and sensibly in all of their responsibilities. Reverence for God is the beginning of wisdom—knowledge of God is the result of living by His wisdom.

Godly wisdom is always consistent with godly character. God does not give gifts impersonally; His greatest gift to us is Himself. "But of him are ye in Christ Jesus, who of God is made unto us wisdom, and righteousness, and sanctification, and redemption (I Corinthians 1:30 KJV)." God's wisdom is inseparable from His righteousness. For God's people, honesty is not only the best policy, it is the only policy.

- 4:11-13 *I would have you learn this great fact: that a life of doing right is the wisest life there Is. If you live that kind of life, you'll not limp or stumble as you run. Carry out my instructions; don't forget them, for they will lead you to real living.*

"But the good man walks along in the ever brightening light of God's favor; the dawn gives way to morning splendor, while the evil man gropes and stumbles in the dark (Proverbs 4:18-19)." "For the Lord watches over all the plans and paths of godly men; but the paths of the godless lead to doom (Psalm 1:6)." "Yet, finally, the innocent shall come out on top, above the godless; the righteous shall move onward and forward; those with pure hearts shall become stronger and stronger (Job 17:8-9)." Living by God's wisdom assures us of God's presence and action in our lives—living by worldly wisdom, or "by our wits" removes us from the place of God's blessing, and brings ultimate failure and condemnation.

Godly wisdom is always consistent with God's design for Creation. What God says is the only reliable statement of how His Creation really works.

Perspective and Attitude

Wars, love, and businesses have all been lost from loss of objectivity and lack of control of attitudes. Always try to see the other person's perspective. Minimize your achievements, maximize the other's. Always say it with a smile, and mean it. Hire people who smile in person and on the phone and on the computer. Don't get into the habit of defending yourself. Even when you know you are right, let it go. Why let pride ruin your chances?

Quiet confidence is essential to the character of God (Exodus 3:14; Isaiah 57:15; Habakkuk 2:20). Jesus has a mindset of humility and willingness to serve (Philippians 2:4-8). If the character of God, as revealed in Christ, is being worked into our lives, our character will epitomize the perspectives of eternity and an attitude of quiet confidence.

According to Proverbs:

• 10:22 *The Lord's blessing is our greatest wealth. All our work adds nothing to it.*

"Fear not ... I am thy shield, and thy exceeding great reward (Genesis 15:1).""We live within the shadow of the Almighty, sheltered by the God who is above all gods (Psalm 91:1)." "The Lord is my Helper and I am not afraid of anything mere man can do to me (Hebrews 13:6)." "What can we ever say to such wonderful things as these? If God is on our side, who can ever be against us (Romans 8:31)?" "But my God shall supply all your need according to his riches in glory by Christ Jesus (Philippians 4:19 KJV)." When God's people walk in God's wisdom, they can depend on God's presence and God's provision. Many people who think they have "arrived" have no idea where they are going.

• 28:25 *Greed causes fighting; trusting in God leads to prosperity.*

"What is causing the quarrels and fights among you? Isn't it because there is a whole army of evil desires within you? You want what you don't have, so you kill to get it. You long for what others have, and can't afford it, so you start a fight to take it away from them. And yet the reason you don't have what you want is that you don't ask God for it (James 4:1-2)." Cut-throat wheeling and dealing and contentious lawsuits have become common business practices. One high-stakes entrepreneur expressed the lawless shrewdness he considered normative: "The feds have been after me for years—they don't understand business." Seeking profit at any cost eventually claims the highest cost—one's own soul (Matthew 16:26). God sustains those who seek His glory and live by His wisdom.

Contentment in God's presence is priceless. "Ambition and death are alike in this: neither is ever satisfied (Proverbs 27:20)." "He who loves money shall never have enough (Ecclesiastes 5:10)." "But godliness with contentment is great gain (I Timothy 6:6 KJV)." God's greatest gift to us is Himself; all other blessings are derived from His presence and activity in our lives. Peace and contentment come from knowing that God is with us.

• 18:11 *The rich man thinks of his wealth as an impregnable defense, a high wall of safety. What a dreamer!*

"…I'll sit back and say to myself, 'Friend, you have enough stored away for years to come. Now take it easy! Wine, women, and song for you!' But God said to him, 'Fool! Tonight you die. Then who will get it all? Yes, every man is a fool who gets rich on earth but not in heaven Luke 12:19-21)." "The thorny ground represents the hearts of people who listen to the Good News and receive it, but all too quickly the attractions of this world and the delights of wealth, and the search for success and lure of nice things come in and crowd out God's message from their hearts, so that no crop is produced (Mark 4:18-19)." When the comforts of this world displace concern for the next world, people are deluded into thinking they have found what they were looking for—but they were looking for riches in all the wrong places.

- 10:30-31 *The good shall never lose God's blessings, but the wicked shall lose everything. The good man gives wise advice, but a liar's counsel is shunned.*

"A man without God is trusting in a spider's web. Everything he counts on will collapse (Job 8:14)." "All who listen to my instructions and follow them are wise, like a man who builds his house on solid rock ... But those who hear my instructions and ignore them are foolish, like a man who builds his house on sand (Matthew 7:24, 26)." "He frustrates the plans of crafty men. They are caught in their own traps; he thwarts their schemes (Job 5:12-13)." "How I hate falsehood but how I love your laws.... Deliver me, O Lord, from liars (Psalm 119:163; 120:2)." The truth of God's wisdom will ultimately prevail—it is foolish to exclude God from our plans. Deceit may bring temporary gains, but honesty wins God's lasting favor.

Security in God's provision is permanent. Markets may rise, fall, or crash, but God carries His people along. The Creator of all things can be trusted to supply all of our real needs. God alone is God—anyone who attempts to find security apart from God is certain to fail.

- 10:2-3 *Ill-gotten gains brings no lasting happiness; right living does. The Lord will not let a good man starve to death, nor will He let the wicked man's riches last forever.*

"Don't you realize that ever since man was first placed upon the earth, the triumph of the wicked has been short-lived, and the joy of the godless but for a moment (Job 20:4-5)." "For these men brag of all their evil lusts; they revile God and congratulate those the Lord abhors, whose only goal in life is money (Psalm 10:3)." "I have been young and now I am old. And in all my years I have never seen the Lord forsake a man who loves him; nor have I seen the children of the godly go hungry (Psalm 37:25)." "Many sorrows come to the wicked, but abiding love surrounds those who trust in the Lord (Psalm 32:10)." Those who devote their lives to gaining money may have their moment in the sun and their "fifteen minutes of fame," but those who devote their lives to God have lasting happiness.

- 11:6 *The good man's goodness delivers him; the evil man's treachery is his undoing.*

"'Sir, Haman has just ordered a 75-foot gallows constructed, to hang Mordecai, the man who saved the king from assassination! It stands in Haman's courtyard.' 'Hang Haman on it," the king ordered (Esther 7:9-10)." "O evil man, leave the upright man alone, and quit trying to cheat him out of his rights. Don't you know that this good man, though you trip him up seven times, will each time rise again? But one calamity is enough to lay you low (Proverbs 24:15-16)." "I look to you for help, O Lord God. You are my refuge. Don't let them slay me. Keep me out of their traps. Let them fall into their own snares, while I escape (Psalm 141:8-10)." Those who follow God's wisdom enjoy God's protection—those who devise wicked schemes will bring about their own destruction.

Departure from God's precepts will be punished. Obedient faith leads to God's blessing. Disobedience falls under His judgment. God has revealed Himself, and He has spoken. It's not as if professed atheism or agnosticism can establish real worldviews. Some people just don't want to think about God, because He would interfere with the way they want to do business (Romans 1:18-23). God cannot be pushed aside—He is still here, and He is still in control. God's commands and guidance provide the only pattern for ultimate success.

• 28:21 *Giving preferred treatment to rich people is a clear case of selling one's soul for a piece of bread.*

"Dear brothers, how can you claim to belong to the Lord Jesus Christ, the Lord of glory, if you show favoritism to rich people and look down on poor people (James 2:1)?" "Never twist justice to benefit a rich man, and never accept bribes. For bribes blind the eyes of the wisest and corrupt their decisions (Deuteronomy 16:19)." Wealth can distort judgment in various ways. Those who have it may be defrauded by those who want it—it becomes difficult to know who is a true friend and who is just looking for material favors. Those who are poorer may be bedazzled by the apparent generosity of those who are richer—their sense of right and wrong may be clouded by their desire for gifts. A whole society may be corrupted by greed—obsession with gaining wealth, and misuse of it once gained.

God's people should never show partiality. "We are no longer Jews or Greeks or slaves or free men or even merely men or women—we are Christians, we are one in Christ Jesus (Galatians 3:28)." Artificial distinctions of background and circumstances carry no weight in God's judgment. We are all finite and sinful, needing to be sustained by God's providence, needing to be saved by His grace.

• 28:11 *Rich men are conceited, but their real poverty is evident to the poor.*

• 16:19 *Better poor and humble than proud and rich*

"You say, 'I am rich, with everything I want; I don't need a thing!' And you don't realize that spiritually you are wretched and miserable and poor and blind and naked (Revelation 3:17)." "Listen to me, dear brothers: God has chosen poor people to be rich in faith, and the Kingdom of Heaven is theirs, for that is the gift God has promised to all those who love him (James 2:5)." It is foolish to gloat over temporary pleasure while failing to gain eternal treasure.

Ingratitude for God's provision breeds pride. "Always remember that it is the Lord your God who gives you power to become rich…. (Deuteronomy 8:18)." In his pride, King Nebuchadnezzar once said," Is not this great Babylon, that I have built for the house of the kingdom by the might of my power, and for the honour of my majesty (Daniel 4:30)?" God immediately took away his kingdom, his palace, and his sanity, leaving Nebuchadnezzar to forage for food like an animal.

• 11:7 *When an evil man dies, his hopes all perish, for they are based upon this earthly life.*

"They spend their days in wealth, and in a moment go down to the grave (Job 21:13 KJV)." "You have spent your years here on earth having fun, satisfying your every whim, and now your fat hearts are ready for the slaughter (James 5:5)." "And I am disgusted about this, that I must leave the fruits of all my hard work to others (Ecclesiastes 2:18)." "Don't store up treasures here on earth where they can erode away or may be stolen. Store them in heaven where they will never lose their value, and are safe from thieves (Matthew 6:19-20)." There is truth in the motto: "Only one life, it will soon be past—only what's done for Christ will last." Some people make sure their wealth will last until the end of their earthly life—but they have made no provision for themselves beyond that. How much did the billionaire leave when he died? All of it. He who dies with the most toys still dies.

Indifference to God's promises brings eternal poverty. Moses "chose to share ill-treatment with God's people instead of enjoying the fleeting pleasures of sin. He thought that it was better to suffer for the promised Christ than to own all the treasures of Egypt, for he was looking forward to the great reward that God would give him (Hebrews 11:25-26)." Paul admitted, "If being a Christian is of value to us only now in this life, we are the most miserable of creatures (I Corinthians 15:19)."

61

Obedient faith looks beyond the temporary comforts of this life, trusting God for blessings both now and for all eternity. Those who seek only worldly wealth find only worldly wealth—they have no treasures, and no place, in Heaven.

- 15:15 *When a man is gloomy, everything seems to go wrong; when he is cheerful, everything seems right.*
- 17:22 *A cheerful heart does good like medicine, but a broken spirit makes one sick.*

"O my soul, why be so gloomy and discouraged? Trust in God! I shall again praise him for his wondrous help; he will make me smile again, for he is my God (Psalm 43:5)!" Attitudes affect action. "My heart wasn't in it" is a well-understood excuse for lackluster performance of any activity. Body language betrays unexpressed emotions. Enthusiasm energizes a person— passion turns any task into a work of art. And emotions are contagious—a whole team can be lifted up or brought down by the attitude of one person.

Inclusion in God's plan brightens our prospects. J. Vernon McGee said that one of his favorite phrases in the Bible was, "It came to pass." Whatever comes our way will pass away eventually. In the midst of the cruelest crisis, we can say, "This is finite." All earthly trials will come to an end. Obedient faith puts one in the place of God's blessing. When the blessing comes, it will be lasting. Being aware of God's presence and activity in our lives puts everything else in perspective. Peace with God sanctifies every earthly conflict (Romans 5:1-5).

Counsel and Criticism

Being critical in marriage is folly and shameful. Ben Franklin said, "Go into marriage with your eyes wide open, then shut them half way." We must also go into our finances and business with our eyes wide open. Listening and soliciting advice and critical analysis in business is useful, helpful, and necessary. Get all the help you can. Listen carefully, then swallow your pride and make the necessary adjustments.

Consultants and "idea people" are a dime a dozen. They will spend other people's money without giving it a thought. Most consultants I have met were those recently released from employment. They didn't know what they were doing when they had their jobs, and now they are exporting their ignorance to any who are foolish enough to hire them. If you want to know how to be successful in any area, ask someone who has been successful in that area or a similar field. If you can't find that person, read his book; he most likely wrote one.

I recently talked with a consultant who was hired to improve an institution's efficiency. They would have been better off investing the money spent on "the team" who had no knowledge of how this type of institution worked. The truth of the matter was that the institution had several well-qualified employees who were willing to help and had a vested interest in its success, yet were never consulted. Always ask your own first; it will be surprising how many times you will solve the "problem" in-house.

For an objective opinion, always consult with your wife before starting a new venture. She has a vested interest in your success, and will give you a straightforward analysis. Don't sell her short; you picked her out from over three-and-one-half-billion potential partners. Only the most insecure, selfish, or foolish man would fail to talk over a financial or business matter with his wife, seeking her suggestions or counsel. Don't expect a "yes man" answer from her. You don't pay her enough for her to not tell you the truth as she perceives it.

It doesn't matter how bright a person thinks he is, or even how bright you think he is; you must know exactly where you are financially at all times. I knew a man who owned several businesses and he always signed every check himself, even though he had good accounting people working for him.

He never wrote a check twice to the same company because it was his money, and he always remembered to whom he had written one! Smart man!

Inventory can be a killer, yet certain people love to order more than necessary. Don't hire them to control inventory. Make sure the inventory person wants the store or warehouse stocked only with high turnover items, no matter what pressure others exert on him or her. I would rather have, as a warehouse commander, a housewife who knows how to plan meals and efficiently run her household on a limited budget than a Harvard business graduate who loves to spend and won't accept criticism.

Some people have the idea that they have all the answers. Always hire the person who knows how to invite suggestions from many sources and is not afraid to say, "I don't know the answer to that right now." The Bible promotes the idea of a life-long learner. The following proverbs encourage us to listen and to ask critical questions of ourselves and of those we trust.

Objectivity is essential to the character of God (Deuteronomy 32:4; Psalm 89:14; Jeremiah 9:23-24). Jesus judges according to absolute truth (Isaiah 11:1-5; John 5:30). If the character of God, as revealed in Christ, is being worked into our lives, our character will epitomize objective response to counsel and criticism.

According to Proverbs:

- 10:8   *The wise man is glad to be instructed, but a self-sufficient fool falls flat on his face.*

"To learn, you must want to be taught. To refuse reproof is stupid (Proverbs 12:1)." "Only a fool despises his father's advice; a wise son considers each suggestion (Proverbs 15:5)." It's amazing how much we can learn if we don't discredit the source. Reporters, detectives, doctors, and mental therapists cannot build their careers on intuitive knowledge — they must ask questions, and accept unexpected answers. Too often, pride keeps us from admitting our areas of ignorance, and we go on pretending that we know what we are doing. Anyone who knows all the answers has not asked all the questions.

"Only fools refuse to be taught (Proverbs 1:7)." Some people think they have "arrived" at a level of spiritual or mental maturity which puts them beyond the need for further instruction. Their training and experience give them a self-assurance which cannot be penetrated by new ideas. Twenty years of experience is too often one year of experience repeated nineteen times, with no lessons learned, and no fresh insights. We can all use more "Aha!" experiences which make us admit, "You learn something new every day!"

- 15:22 *Plans go wrong with too few counselors; many counselors bring success*
- 20:18a *Don't go ahead with your plans, without the advice of others.*
- 12:26 *A good man asks advice from friends; the wicked plunge ahead and fall.*
- 19:20a *Get all the advice you can.*

"A fool thinks he needs no advice, but a wise man listens to others (Proverbs 12:15)." The quotation attributed to missionary/explorer David Livingstone is quite true: "Adventures are a sign of poor planning." Poor planning does not adequately prepare for obstacles and challenges which are likely to arise. Two (or more) heads are better than one because different people bring different perspectives which contribute to balanced, comprehensive planning. We all have blind spots which may be exactly where another person's vision is clearest.

"Pride goes before destruction and haughtiness before a fall (Proverbs 16:18)." Nobody could say "I told you so" after a disaster if we had paid attention when they first told us. "He just wouldn't listen" has told the story of many failures. "Before every man there lies a wide and pleasant road he thinks is right, but it ends in death (Proverbs 16:25)." Individualism, self-sufficiency, and bold action can bring marvelous success—or tragic calamity. Those who are driven to live in fame are at high risk of going down in flames, if they don't listen to the people around them.

- 25:12 *It is a badge of honor to accept valid criticism.*
- 13:18 *If you refuse criticism, you will end in poverty and disgrace; if you accept criticism, you are on the road to fame.*
- 15:31, 32 *If you profit from constructive criticism, you will be elected to the wise man's hall of fame. But to reject criticism is to harm yourself and your own best interests.*
- 23:12 *Don't refuse to accept criticism; get all the help you can.*

"It is better to be criticized by a wise man than to be praised by a fool! (Ecclesiastes 7:5)." "...If the Lord has told him to curse me, who am I to say no? And perhaps the Lord will see that I am being wronged and will bless me because of these curses (II Samuel 16:10, 12)." Leaders tend to attract yes-men, "groupies" who gravitate toward positions of perceived power. Even "accountability groups" can become self-perpetuating mutual admiration societies, where sympathy and camaraderie take precedence over candid confrontation. Criticism from a reputable source may be sharp enough to hurt, yet accurate enough to help. Even malicious criticism may include a grain of truth, or at least challenge us to make sure it is not true.

Many of us have found that our greatest strengths can become our greatest weaknesses. Confident in the things we do well, we think we are "golden," and that we can do no wrong. In the Church, the body of Christ, there is diversity in unity—each member has unique abilities and opportunities (I Corinthians 12; Ephesians 4). If three people think exactly alike, two of them are not thinking. We all need people who can cover our blind spots, seeing what we might like to overlook. We should not let our reactions to the motives of criticism interfere with honest response to the truthful content of criticism.

Conduct

Character determines conduct.

What we do flows from what we are. If our moral compass spins in response to shifting cultural norms, our actions will be as inconsistent as our values. If our values are anchored in unchanging truth, our actions will be truthful, dependable, and considerate. Faith in God's wisdom produces faithfulness in human action.

Daniel's Dynasty

Daniel had an eclectic education. He was among the Jewish youths selected to be trained for Nebuchadnezzar's court. His qualifications included having been highly educated already in Israel, and being capable of learning Chaldean language and literature—becoming so thoroughly knowledgeable that he could become one of the King's counselors. A brilliant young man, advancing to the highest intellectual attainments available in two distinct cultures. It's easy to get stuck with the image of Daniel as a brilliant young man daring to stand alone in His obedience to God amidst the attacks of a pagan society. The lion's den, the fiery furnace his friends endured, the hand-writing on the wall, the dramatic prophecies of the end times—the book of Daniel is full of Sunday school stories and eschatological wonders. It's easy to miss the chronology of Daniel's life. By the end of the book, he was an old man.

So what happened? History often deals with dynasties, rulers establishing hereditary control of a nation, passing the throne from generation to generation. Daniel outlived several attempts to establish such a dynasty over the land where he lived. Kings came and went, suffering court intrigues, temporary insanity, and foreign invasion. In fact, the foreigners were victorious, killing the sitting king and taking over the throne. All this in the lifetime of one man—Daniel.

What was Daniel doing? Here's the story which should be among the most memorable impressions of the book of Daniel. Kings would rise and fall. Their dynasties were never secured. But Daniel, the captive from Israel, went on doing what he had been doing, counseling the kings. The only man who stayed at the center of power was Daniel, God's man. Daniel had his own one-man dynasty going—whoever was on the throne, whichever culture dominated, there was Daniel, giving solid counsel.

How could he do that? The United Nations, or any individual nation, would be glad to have the services of a diplomat who could maintain his own core convictions while translating excellent practical wisdom cross-culturally. He absorbed everything he could from the broadest and deepest learning of the dominant culture, yet never compromised the eternal wisdom of God. This would be a remarkable achievement in any time or place—including our own. Can we do it?

What we do determines our effectiveness.

Being the right kind of person doesn't pay the rent or buy the groceries. We need street smarts to make life work. Not the worldly wisdom of shrewdness, self-promotion, and ruthless opportunism, but conscientious diligent effort to be effective. Responsibility will characterize our work ethic; respect will characterize our relationships.

Responsibility in our work

Responsibility is the ability (and willingness) to respond correctly to reasonable expectations. Being the "go to person" in any matter means being the person who can be depended on to get the job done quickly and completely. That's being responsible. How do you get that way? It's not enough to be the first volunteer. Eagerness has to be fortified by information and implemented by sustained effort. Responsible people know what the job requires, and think of the best way to get it done. They are willing to put their own time and energy into making sure plans are carried out effectively.

I heard of a man who began his business career at age seventeen, mowing lawns in his neighborhood. When his own hard work had built up a clientele, he recruited four friends who owned trucks, and gave each of them a mower and a list of customers. He kept working himself, making sure the workers were well-equipped, and checking with customers to be sure they were satisfied with the work. When he moved on to further his education, he gave the business to several young relatives, who were not as diligent as he was. They frittered away the profits, neglected the clients, and were surprised when the workers quit, taking the business with them. Responsibility earns rewards; irresponsibility wastes resources

---

Adam's Apples

The lump in a man's throat is nicknamed "Adam's apple," suggesting that the first man had a hard time swallowing the Forbidden Fruit. Whatever we think of the Tree of the Knowledge of Good and Evil, the Garden of Eden must have had something like apple trees; the whole gene pool of all Creation was there. Adam's original job was to take care of the garden. His first responsibility was to make himself useful by making his surroundings fruitful. Productive work was not part of the curse for sin. The curse came later, and involved the effects of Adam's sin on his environment. The Creation suffered consequences of sin which made productive work much more difficult (Romans 8:19-23; Genesis 3:17-10).

Adam was the best man for the job. Naming all the animals showed incredible intelligence and understanding. He understood the animals well enough to differentiate their characteristics, and to give each kind an appropriate title. It is easy for us to overlook the fact that Adam was a linguist, as well as a naturalist. Nominalization, the giving of names, is the foundation of language formation. Besides identifying the animals for his own reference, he was creating a base vocabulary for human communication. Working with his hands, he maintained a beautiful garden; working with his mind, he formed a clear and accurate language. Adam was a busy man.

Work, in itself, is not a curse, but a blessing. God's commission to Adam and Eve is repeated (with significant variation) to Noah and his sons. Humans are to "subdue" Creation, bringing order and arrangement, and to "replenish" Creation, bringing beauty and fruitfulness. We are all to tend God's garden, not just our own little corner of it. To the best of our physical and mental abilities, we are to make ourselves useful in productive work. If we want to eat apples, we'll have to take care of the apple trees.

Planning

Romans 12:3-8 tells believers to assess their gifts and opportunities realistically, and to do what God gives them to do diligently and conscientiously. If our bodies belong to God, and our minds have been changed by His Word, we can expect His guidance and blessing as we "plan our work, and work our plan."

Some people lack clear goals, refuse to take the time and effort for short-term or long-term planning, then blame the Lord for their own foolishness and failure. Ninety-five percent of successful business people have both short and long-term goals in written form, and review them at least yearly (the other five percent also have goals; they are just so smart they don't have to write them down).

Many new businesses fail within the first few years. Most of these are goalless, and most have not sought wise counsel before embarking on their failure excursion. God warns us to get counsel from wise people and draw detailed plans, while trusting Him for the results. A great man of faith, George Mueller, said, "Plan and work like it all depends on you and pray like it all depends on Him."

Sometimes the need to change plans arises. Don't be stubborn or prideful when the plan isn't working. No matter what the investment in time or energy is, give it up and draw up a new one. Remember Who the Boss really is and Whose money is at stake.

Cookies or Cans?

It doesn't take an MBA to form a good business plan—or to change direction when something better comes up. When I was a head resident at the University of Arkansas, my two daughters asked for an allowance. I told them that there were over 17,000 students at the university, and that if they couldn't get some of the students' money into their pockets, they didn't understand the free enterprise system! Melissa, the oldest, built up a clientele of students who bought cookies from her during their study breaks. She slaved over a hot stove for hours to create her products—until her little sister Sarah's business blossomed. Sarah simply marked some boxes, "Sarah's Cans," and put some on each dormitory floor for collection of returnable beverage cans. Twice a month, she emptied the boxes into plastic trash bags and took them to the recycling center. Her income surpassed Melissa's profits with much lower demands on time and effort. Sarah cut Melissa into her business as a forty-percent partner, and assigned her to the upper floors.

My good friend, Don, read in the Scriptures that "you should plant your field before building your house." He did what the Bible said, and with his first cash crop of his blueberries, he built his home for cash.

Keep a close eye on trends, and on all your business interests. Don't depend on anyone but God or you will surely be sorry. Carefully guard these biblical "secrets" and see your interests flourish.

The first thing almost all successful people do in the morning is to make their bed. It is the first task and their first victory.

Order and arrangement are essential to the work of God (Isaiah 46:9-11; Ecclesiastes 3:11; Acts 17:24-26). Jesus lived, died, and rose again according to God's plan (John 4:34; Acts 2:23-24). If the work of God, as revealed in Christ, is being worked into our lives, our work will epitomize careful planning.

According to Proverbs:

- 24:3,4 *Any enterprise is built by wise planning, becomes strong through common sense and profits wonderfully by keeping abreast of the facts.*
- 20:18 *Don't go ahead with your plans without the advice of others.*
- 24:27 *Develop your business before building your house.*

"For who would begin construction of a building without first getting estimates and then checking to see if he has enough money to pay the bills? Otherwise he might complete only the foundation before running out of funds. And then how everyone would laugh (Luke 14:38-39)." A dream is not a plan until it is translated into nuts and bolts and dollars and cents. Start-up costs for a small business must include the length of time the business will be in operation before it becomes profitable. Profits cannot be spent until they are made, and re-investment in the business should take priority over personal spending (house, car, boat). Building a business may require a simpler lifestyle for a long time before it makes a more comfortable lifestyle possible.

The great missionary, explorer, and naturalist Livingstone once said, "Adventures are a sign of poor planning." Good planning establishes priorities, covers contingencies, and is open to necessary adjustment. If a good idea can be represented by a light bulb over one's head, good planning puts the bulb into a fixture and connects it to the power.

- 27:12a *A sensible man watches for problems ahead and prepares to meet them.*
- 14:16 *A wise man is cautious and avoids danger; a fool plunges ahead with great confidence.*
- 14:8 *The wise man looks ahead; the fool attempts to fool himself and won't face the facts.*
- 13:16 *A wise man thinks ahead; a fool doesn't, and even brags about it!*

"But those who hear my instructions and ignore them are foolish, like a man who build his house on sand. For when the rains and floods come, and storm winds beat against his house, it will fall with a mighty crash (Matthew 7:26-27)."Dreamers see only their goals—planners see how to reach them. Most worthwhile achievements are accomplished at some risk. Since we all want to believe the most optimistic prospects for our plans, it is wise to seek the counsel of others who can show us the negative points we would like to ignore. A good plan is only as good as its provision for bad possibilities.

Lemmings are simple little animals whose greatest claim to fame is their supposed mass migration to death. "If your friends told you to jump off a cliff, would you do it?" Well, maybe if they did. Running with a crowd can be exhilarating, but it has its risks. Ignoring danger can be catastrophic. Nobody on the plane is reassured when the pilot says, "We can't tell where we are or what direction we're going—but we're making good time."

- 18:13 *What a shame—yes, how stupid! – to decide before knowing the facts.*
- 19:2 *It is dangerous and sinful to rush into the unknown.*

- 13:19 *It is pleasant to see plans develop. That is why fools refuse to give them up even when they are wrong. (Be flexible).*

"A fool thinks he needs no advice, but a wise man listens to others (Proverbs 12:15)." Fools rush in—and don't know when it's time to get out. Making hasty decisions, and proudly defending them against common sense leads to disaster. If the truth were known, "Plan A" hardly ever succeeds without significant modifications. Stonewalling in the face of mounting evidence leads to failure and disgrace.

Lack of planning is foolish; rigidity in planning can be just as bad. "The Charge of the Light Brigade" and the Bay of Pigs invasion are just two examples of disastrous implementation of inadequate military plans. Many employees know that the only way to convince the boss that he's wrong is to do exactly what he says. The most elegant plans must not be valued more highly than common sense about updated information about changes in the real-world situation (i.e., Lemmings don't really follow each other off cliffs, but people often fail at things that others have failed at because they lacked common sense and didn't do due diligence in preparation for their idea.).

- 27:1 *Don't brag about your plans for tomorrow. Wait and see what happens.*
- 16:9 *We should make plans-counting on God to direct us*
- 16:1 *We can make our plans, but the final outcome is in God's hands.*
- 19:21 *Man proposes but God disposes.*

"Look here, you people who say, 'Today or tomorrow we are going to such and such a town, stay there a year, and open up a profitable business.' How do you know what is going to happen tomorrow? For the length of your lives is as uncertain as the morning fog—now you see it; soon it is gone. What you ought to say is, 'If the Lord wants us to, we shall live and do this or that (James 4:13-15)." The best laid plans of men and women are, at best, the plans of men and women. The plan of God supersedes, and may cancel, any plans we make.

We all know what happens to the best laid plans. If somebody doesn't prove they're not foolproof, something will happen which throws us off course. Even the apostle Paul had to change his mission plans under God's direction (Acts 16:6-10)."

Hard Work

While the Reformation countries flourished financially with their Protestant Christian work ethic, as did the Puritans in America, those countries that continued religious oppression and stole from their fellow countrymen in the name of the church, a creed, or a tyrant dwindled, and continue to suffer today. The former Soviet Union plowed and planted by the "book" no matter what the weather. Farm workers plowed and planted in three feet of mud because the tyrant said so, and they had no ability, authority, or incentive to make independent decisions. In such a system, even hard work cannot bring good results from poor planning.

The poor can starve because some ignorant madman makes up a religious lie, and says they can't eat certain meats or kill the rats that eat the grain. A nation can steal incentive from its population through unfair taxation or through robbing the poor by giving them subsistence living without requiring work or offering hope of a better future. In the end, such policies bring only laziness and despair. Keeping children out of the work force until they are sixteen years old (because a former generation abused and exploited the young) is a sure way to promote a generation of sloths.

The Bible gives instruction and warnings concerning bad government, bad theology, bad parenting, and bad living. Good planning must be made effective through hard work.

Persistence towards completion is essential to the work of God (Numbers 23:19; Philippians 1:6). Jesus did not let personal discomfort or fear of opposition, or personnel deter him from accomplishing His purpose on earth (Luke 9:51; Matthew 26:39). If the work of God, as revealed in Christ, is being worked into our lives, our work will epitomize consistent effort.

According to Proverbs:

• 16:26 *Hunger is good – if it makes you work to satisfy it.*

"In the sweat of thy face shalt thou eat bread… (Genesis 3:19)." "…we never accepted food from anyone without buying it; we worked hard day and night for the money to live on…. We wanted to show you, firsthand, how you should work for a living…. We gave you this rule: 'He who does not work shall not eat (II Thessalonians 3:8-12)." Basic physical needs motivate us to work. Paul made himself an example of hard-working provision for one's own needs. Everyone who is able to work should work.

"A lazy man sleeps soundly – and goes hungry (Proverbs 19:15)!" There will always be people who deserve help because of disability or disaster, but the world doesn't owe anyone a living. Everyone owes the world an honest effort to be productive, and to help meet the legitimate needs of others. Nobody gets a free ride. Inheritance or government-recognized entitlement may tempt some to sit back and take their ease, but "earning one's keep" brings the satisfaction of purposeful living. It is commendable that many who are the beneficiaries of "old money" have devoted their lives to public service. For most of us, our needs constitute a call to work hard to meet them.

• 12:11 *Hard work means prosperity; only a fool idles away his time.*

• 21:5 *Steady plodding brings prosperity; hasty speculation brings poverty.*

• 28:19 *Hard work brings prosperity, playing around brings poverty.*

"Take a lesson from the ants, you lazy fellow. Learn from their ways and be wise! For though they have no king to make them work, yet they labor hard all summer, gathering food for the winter (Proverbs 6:6-8)." Even ants are self-motivated to work hard in order to survive. Their steady effort builds the resources they need. There is no substitute for hard work—hoping to win the lottery or to rake in the profits of a get-rich-quick scheme will not buy the groceries this week.

Laziness might be pictured as a person lying in a hammock, sipping lemonade. A more accurate picture would be of someone leaning on a shovel or broom, or leaning back in a desk chair.

The person in the hammock isn't even pretending to work. Lazy people are ready to look busy if the boss shows up. Conscientious workers are self-motivated, and stay on task even without direct supervision. It's a matter of character, and it shows. Good workers maintain a consistent level of activity, and follow the most logical steps to get the job done. Besides the rewards of a clear conscience and the respect of others, they enjoy a secondary benefit—looking busy is often harder work than actually being busy.

- 27:18   *A workman may eat from the orchard he tends; anyone should be rewarded who protects another's interest.*
- 14:4   *An empty stable stays clean – but there is no income from an empty stable.*

"For the Scriptures say, 'Never tie up the mouth of an ox when it is treading out the grain—let him eat as he goes along!' And in another place, 'Those who work deserve their pay (I Timothy 5:18)!'" "Know the state of your flocks and herds; 25,26,27 then there will be lamb's wool enough for clothing, and goat's milk enough for food for all your household (Proverbs 27:23-27)." Being a good steward of another's capital or re-investing in one's own business will bring well-deserved rewards

- 20:4   *If you won't plow in the cold, you won't eat in the harvest.*

"... Does a farmer always plow and never sow? Is he forever harrowing the soil and never planting it? Does he not finally plant his many kinds of grain, each in its own section of his land (Isaiah 28:23-25)?" Hard work includes the drudgery of doing the groundwork for future success. In farming, preparation of the ground can be tiring work, and often must be done in bad weather. But if the uncomfortable work of preparation is neglected, every stage of the crop's growth is affected, and the harvest will be diminished. In spiritual life or in business the same principle is true—the sometimes unpleasant spadework must be done in order to assure ultimate success.

> Life is Just a Bowl of Berries—If You Work Hard
>
> The fallacy of the get-rich-quick attitude is double-edged. Getting rich is not a big enough goal to satisfy human needs for identity and relationship, and those who get rich seldom do it quickly. My son Jacob was eleven years old when he wanted to open a skateboard shop. After discussing child labor laws, inventory requirements and overhead expenses for about an hour, he agreed that his skateboard shop would not be profitable. He decided to become a blueberry farmer on some land we owned. A good friend was knowledgeable and successful in raising blueberries, and counseled us concerning water systems, weeding, fertilizer, bird problems, and other considerations. We took a university extension course on pruning and plant care, and decided the project required time and hard work—which we were willing to invest. There was plenty of labor in preparing the land and transplanting two acres of full-grown plants. When his first crop came in, Jacob repaid the loan I had given him for the plants, and gave the rest of his money to missions. This was one young man who learned that get-to-work-quick-and-keep-working was the only sure way to financial success. His giving to missions showed his commitment to use his resources unselfishly.

• 14:11 *The work of the wicked will perish; the work of the godly will flourish.*

"Unless the Lord builds a house, the builders' work is useless. Unless the Lord protects a city, sentries do no good (Psalm 127:1)." Temporary success and temporary comfort are the highest attainments of people without God. God's people find earthly contentment and eternal joy by including God in all their plans and efforts.

No Laziness

"As in a standing pool, worms and filthy creepers increase, so do evil and corrupt thoughts in an idle person." "From the same materials one man builds a palace, another a hovel." Idleness "is the bane of body and mind, and the nurse of naughtiness, the chief mother of all mischief, one of the seven deadly sins, the Devil's cushion, his pillow and chief reposal… an idle dog will be mangy and how shall an idle person escape?" "Idleness of the mind is much worse than that of the body; wit without employment is a disease, the rust of the soul, a plague and hell itself." (*How to Get on in the World*, by Major Calhoun).

Choose your workers with care, and set a sterling example to all, both in work and character. Remember, "Reputation is what people believe about us, character is what we really are," and,

"Adversity is the best test of character as it is of friendship."

"Early to bed early to rise, makes a man healthy, wealthy, and wise." B. Franklin.

"Rise early, and be an economist of time. Maintain dignity." Bishop Middleton.

No one in the Bible was ever commended for staying up late, but there are many commendations for those who rose early, from the prophets to the domestic worker, and the example of the Lord Himself. Most people spend one-third of their life in a death-like state: sleep. Learn the secret of sleeping less and working more. Interrupting your sleep won't take time away from your family. Most men require between three-and-one-half to four hours of sleep per night, the time it takes to go through the rapid eye movement sleep cycle. Women need between five and six-and-a-half hours per night; the rest is fluff. It's like the man in Proverbs 26:14 who turns on his bed like the door on its hinges. Imagine what you could produce with four hours more in each day!

Watchful diligence is essential to the work of God (Psalm 121:3-4; Psalm 66:7). Jesus sometimes worked all day and prayed all night because of a sense of the urgency of His mission (Luke 6:12; John 9:4). If the work of God, as revealed in Christ, is being worked into our lives, our work will epitomize energetic commitment.

According to Proverbs:

- 10:26 *A lazy fellow is a pain to his employers—like smoke In their eyes or vinegar that sets the teeth on edge.*
- 25:19 *Putting confidence in an unreliable man is like chewing with a sore tooth or running with a broken foot.*

"The sluggard is wiser in his own conceit than seven men that can render a reason (Proverbs 26:16)." "There is one thing worse than a fool, and that is a man who is conceited (Proverbs 26:12)." People who have a high opinion of themselves often have a low opinion of work. They may have contempt for their current employment: "This is beneath me—I've got to get out of this dump." They think the world owes them a living, or at least that they can get by with the least possible effort. Never catching the vision of their employer's goals, they look out for their own comfort. Their laziness minimizes their productivity, and poisons the morale of co-workers. Strangely enough, they take perverted pride in their lack of accomplishment.

A lazy man and his job are soon parted—or should be. The best person for any job is the person who can be counted on to get it done with minimal supervision. Micromanagement is a necessary reaction to sloppy work. A supervisor's time is valuable, and is best spent in planning and coordinating work. A worker who needs constant prodding and correction is worse than worthless, because he wastes the boss's time as well as his own. Co-workers catch on, too; if Lazybones doesn't carry a fair share of the workload, somebody will have to make up the difference, or everybody will be tempted to slack off.

- **23:25-26** *The lazy man longs for many things but his hands refuse to work. He is greedy to get, while the godly love to give.*
- **26:13-14** *The lazy man won't go out and work. "There may be a lion outside!" he says. He sticks to his bed like a door does its hinges!*
- **12:9** *It is better to get your hands dirty—and eat—than to be too proud to work and starve.*

"This should be your ambition: to live a quiet life, minding your own business and doing your own work, just as we told you before. As a result, people who are not Christians will trust and respect you, and you will not need to depend on others for enough money to pay your bills (I Thessalonians 4:11-12)." "The man who works hard sleeps well whether he eats little or much… (Ecclesiastes 5:12)." Working to get what we need is far more satisfying than scheming to get what we want. Lazy people want the rewards of work without the work.

Workaholics throw themselves into their work so completely that they have little time or energy to enjoy the fruits of their labor. Loafaholics want the fruits without the labor. Mockingbirds settle into nests other birds have built; lazy people want all the privileges and perks that others have earned through hard work. Godliness with contentment is great gain— laziness with discontentment is great loss.

- **20:13** *If you love sleep, you will end in poverty. Stay awake, work hard, and there will be plenty to eat.*
- **6:10-11** *"Let me sleep a little longer!" Sure just a little more! And as you sleep, poverty creeps upon you like a robber and destroys you; want attacks you in full armor.*
- **24:32-34** *I learned this lesson: a little extra sleep, a little slumber, a folding of the hands to rest—means that poverty will break in upon you suddenly like a robber, and violently like a bandit.*
- **10:5** *A wise youth makes hay while the sun shines, but what a shame to see the lad who sleeps away his hour of opportunity.*

Sleep is like death in that it removes us from the pressure of the activities, relationships, and responsibilities of our daily lives. Some people want to be free of such pressure at all times—their desire for sleep is really a desire to escape the challenges of productive living. They might as well be dead literally, as well as "dead to the world" figuratively. Our mothers warned us of this danger: "Get up, sleepyhead! Are you going to sleep your life away?" Success comes to those who are alert to opportunities to work towards worthy goals.

"Be alert—this country needs more lerts!" Too many people who say, "I could do this job in my sleep!" are not exaggerating by much. If they work at all, their minds are on the day off, the weekend, the vacation, or just what's for dinner, and when can I get my nap? They want a life of ease, where they can kick back and relax. A life of gain without pain. Opportunity sometimes knocks softly—few people ever get the "big break" that launches a fantastic career. Those who bet their lives on winning the lottery forget that millions of dollars in prizes require millions of losers who get no return on their investment. So we have to be alert to opportunities, and we have to work hard to maximize their benefits. Being asleep at the switch, physically or figuratively, can lead to disaster. It never leads to success.

- 12:24 *Work harder and become a leader; be lazy and never succeed.*
- 10:4 *Lazy men are soon poor; hard workers get rich.*

Hard work is satisfying in itself; yet, beyond its material rewards, it gains the respect of other people. Even among the super-rich, those who earned wealth by providing valuable products and services are more honorable than those who gained wealth through shrewdness. Lazy people are too self-centered to make the effort needed to attain either riches or good reputation.

- 16:27 *Idle hands are the devil's workshop; idle lips are his mouthpiece.*

"The heart is the most deceitful thing there is, and desperately wicked. No one can really know how bad it is (Jeremiah 17:9)!" "For from within, out of men's hearts, come evil thoughts of lust, theft, murder, adultery, wanting what belongs to others, wickedness, deceit, lewdness, envy, slander, pride, and all other folly (Mark 7:21-22)."

Seeking one's own comfort by avoiding hard work leaves one open to great evil. Self-centeredness destroys self-control. What is inside comes out, without restraint. If our thoughts and energy are not focused on worthy goals, they may be quickly diffused among a multitude of evils. In the game of life, as in most sports, spectators do not have the self-discipline of active participants, and are likely to express themselves in extreme behavior and speech.

Joseph's Jobs

Joseph's brothers called him a dreamer, but his work ethic helped make his dreams come true. The little brother who dreams of ruling the world can be an insufferable brat. Nobody likes a megalomaniac—they're just afraid to say so. Joseph's brothers weren't afraid to tell him what they thought of him. Even his father was taken aback when Joseph's dreams implied that the whole family, including the parents, would be subject to Joseph's rule. (Genesis 37:1-10).

When the dreamer's brothers caught him alone, away from the protection of their father, they debated about what to do with him. Killing him would have eliminated the irritation, but there might be a problem of conscience, not to mention consequences. So they sold him to slave traders who took him to a far country. They made up a story about how he was killed by wild animals, and that was that—or so they thought. (Genesis 37:11-35).

The slave traders sold Joseph to an Egyptian official. Whatever entry-level job Joseph started with, before long his conscientious work and consistently good results got the boss's attention, and he was promoted. Good deal. Manager of the whole household of one of the prominent men of the land. Later, in Europe, such a major domo would evolve into what we now call "the mayor." Anyway, Joseph had risen quickly to a coveted position in Egyptian society. He had it made—or so he might have thought. (Genesis 37:36; 39:1-6).

Joseph wasn't just an excellent manager. He was such a good-looking young man that the boss's wife took an extracurricular interest in him. When he rejected her advances, she had him fired. Actually, her accusations could have led to his execution, but her husband apparently wasn't completely blind, and Joseph was simply put into prison. (Genesis 39:7-20).

That might have been the end of the story, but two things changed that. Joseph continued trusting God, and accepted his place in the prison so well that he eventually took charge of the place. His attitude and actions were so positive that the warden kept giving him responsibilities until nothing happened in the jail without Joseph's oversight. The inmate had taken over the prison. The other thing that happened was that dream thing, again. This time it was two prisoners who dreamed, and God gave Joseph the interpretations of their dreams. One of them promised to put in a good word for Joseph if his dream turned out as well as Joseph said it would. He forgot, of course. So there Joseph sat in the jail—a respected leader of men, but still in jail. (Genesis 39:21-40:23).

When Pharaoh had some disturbing dreams, Joseph's former fellow-prisoner finally remembered his promise. Joseph was called to the palace, and interpreted the dreams as predictions of severe fluctuations in the economy. Obviously, the government would have to step in with some kind of program to stabilize production and consumption for the coming good and bad times. Who were they going to call? As Pharaoh weighed the seriousness of the situation, Joseph was standing right in front of him. (Genesis 41:1-44).

Cut to the end—when Joseph's brothers had to go to Egypt to get food, they had to bow to the governor of Egypt, their little brother, the dreamer. Joseph had maintained his consistent obedient faith through thick and thin (quite literally), and all his dreams came true.

A Cause for Clunkers

Pessimists think that a good work ethic passed from the scene a few generations ago, when someone first said, "You just can't get good help any more." Many young people now might lament, "You just can't get good parents any more." Career-driven, pleasure-seeking parents have little time or energy to be the adults in their homes. Divorce further complicates matters—effectively taking one parent out of the scene, and leaving the other's parenting credibility seriously impaired. Kids are left to raise themselves, picking up lessons from each other's experiences. Who cares about planning when life is so chaotic, anyway? Why work hard when there is such a high risk of failure?

Can planning and hard work be taught? An essential part of a good work ethic is delayed gratification—being willing to wait for the rewards of one's efforts. Young people are easily distracted by more immediate pleasures. If they have not learned a good work ethic at home, or have rejected it to seize their day of easy amusements, how can they brought back to reality? If delayed gratification motivates a good work ethic, what do young people want that would require planning and hard work?

To every unmotivated teenager a chance to own their own car. What is the catch? They have to restore it.

Two very different Christian men, a factory worker and a bakery manager both had a passion and some useful skills.The passion was to help troubled teens grow spiritually, the skills were knowledge of rebuilding engines and refurbishing old cars. They took their collective skills and passion and funded a ministry for at risk teens.

A small group of teens come to their home made garage. In the side yard they have a collection, or rather an assortment of old cars, "real clunkers" The teens are then paired with the auto of their choice and the lessons begin. The rules are simple, no cursing, drinking or drugs on the premises or off—any violations will put them back on the street with just their feet.

The new "class" of teens starts at the bottom with brooms and dust pans, cleaning the floors and picking up oily rags. They scavenge for parts in various junk yards. They label and stock the parts on shelves they have built. While getting into the habit of working hard, they see the progress others are making, and gather ideas for their own automotive projects.

When they have survived the initiation period, they are promoted to helping those who are further along in the program. Working on welding, sanding, bonding, cleaning, carpeting, installing, rebuilding, and painting they are mentored in skills they can use on their own car—skills which will be marketable as they seek employment.

After helping others, they take their turn to work with others on their own cars. Each directs the work on his own car with the advice of the mentors. They evaluate the car, determining what will need to be done to get it running well and looking good. Then they decide where to start—what needs to be done first, and in what order each other job will follow. What tools will we need today? Do we have the parts we want to put in tomorrow? Who is best at doing that job? Trying to make the most efficient use of material and personnel, the teens learn valuable planning skills which can be transferred to other life (and employment) situations.

Over a sixteen month period, these teens are discipled in the faith as they are mentored in each part of the learning process about restoration of vehicles. Halfway through the course, they began to instruct the new incoming class. This reinforces what they have learned, and develops leadership skills. When they complete the program, some are chosen to show their cars, giving them the satisfaction of a job well done. All enjoy the benefits of ownership and are spiritually richer for the experience.

Those who finish have a car they have built from scratch to showroom clean. Their motivation to own a car has shown them how easy the yoke is when you are working toward a prized goal. The joy of ownership is increased by the pride of accomplishment and the confidence of having become a skilled and disciplined craftsman.

They learn valuable life lessons as well as marketable skills: 1) He that is faithful in little things will be given more. 2)

Help others before helping yourself. 3) Take turns. 4) Teamwork can get the job done quicker and better. 5) Rewards come for services rendered. 6) Grace covers a multitude of sins — mistakes can be corrected if they are admitted.

Those who do finish (most finish) leave with a feeling of accomplishment and achievement. They have grown spiritually, and have become willing to help others. They have been mentored and have mentored. They have gained skill in welding, bodywork, upholstery, detailing, painting, Installation of stereos, and carpet work. These skills, and the leadership qualities they have developed, can put them into business or through college.

Can planning and hard work be taught? Maybe not, but they can be caught where their value is made clear.

These two brothers in Christ, disciples of the word and mentors of the work, will most likely never appear on any Fortune Five Hundred list, but they do what is in their hands to do and lay up treasures in heaven where they really count. Some might consider this ministry small or insignificant, but those who finish the course don't feel that way and neither do their grateful parents and with God there are no little people and no little places.

Respect for others
Speech

James 3 warns that what we say and how we say it can make the difference between blessing and disaster. Christ-like character and godly wisdom set the standard for a biblical approach to business communication. Unlike many leadership decrees, godly wisdom does not always come in non-negotiable pronouncements from on high:

The wisdom that comes from heaven is first of all pure and full of quiet gentleness. Then it is peace-loving and courteous. It allows discussion and is willing to yield to others; it is full of mercy and good deeds. It is wholehearted and straightforward and sincere. And those who are peacemakers will plant seeds of peace and reap a harvest of goodness (James 3:17-18).

Godly wisdom is pure, clean and reverent even when dealing with the complex details of a potentially controversial issue. It is counterproductive to quibble over minor differences, but it is essential to glean enough accurate information to have a clear picture of the major problems a business faces. .

Godly wisdom is characterized by quiet gentleness. It is not bombastic or unkind, even when dealing with rebellious, contentious people. A Christian leader must be unshockable, unshakeable and calm. Jesus almost always spoke tenderly even to grievous sinners. Gentleness is not weakness; Peter's denial of Christ was strongly rebuked by a gentle look from his Lord.

Godly wisdom is peace-loving and courteous. God's grace is not incompatible with common social graces. Peace with God brings inner peace and peaceful relationships with others, even in the midst of trials (Romans 5:1-5). The gospel is God's word of reconciliation, which is the core message of our ministry of reconciliation (II Corinthians 5:18-21). The patience of a person who is at peace with God is displayed in courtesy towards others. Social graces are simply learned behaviors which have proven useful in preserving harmony in human relationships. Christians should model gracious behavior which others can learn to imitate in relating to each other.

Godly wisdom allows discussion and is willing to yield. This is far from the selfish attitude which says, "O.K., I'll listen to your idiotic opinion, but don't expect me to change my mind." A major facet of the biblical concept of repentance is changing one's mind. Transformation into Christ-like character is triggered by renewal of the mind (Romans 12:2). Non-negotiable demands short-circuit profitable communication.

True discussion gives a fair hearing to opposing views and seeks consensus on essential points. Willingness to yield when faced with convincing facts is evidence of true reasonableness. Willingness to yield when faced with pain caused to another is evidence of true love.

Godly wisdom is full of mercy and good deeds. There is a subtle distinction here. Mercy acts to benefit the undeserving as well as the weak, and treats others kindly regardless of their character and actions. The focus of mercy is primarily on the needs of others. Good deeds (good fruit, KJV) express good character—they are natural products of godly wisdom. Believers are "created in Christ Jesus unto good works (Ephesians 2:10)," and demonstrate their faith by helping others. Mercy disregards the character of those it serves; good deeds display the character of those who do them. Being considerate and helpful shows conformity to Christ.

Godly wisdom is wholehearted, straightforward and sincere. There is no deception, no manipulation, and no hypocrisy. In the early history of the Church there was controversy over how the value of the means of grace (preaching, baptism, serving the Lord's Supper, pastoral care) was affected by the character of the person who administered them. In serious communication, there can be no question that the credibility of what is said is inextricably bound to the integrity of the person who says it. Biblical standards of integrity and openness apply to our business practices as well as to our personal lives.

Godly wisdom sows seeds of peace and reaps a harvest of goodness. A ministry of reconciliation heals relationships without compromising either truth or love. Speaking the truth in love brings the peace which only righteousness engenders. Being right with God makes it possible to make things really right with other people. Conversely, seeds of peace bring a harvest of goodness as peace with God frees people to act righteously toward others. Godly communication does not beat people over the head with scathing accusations, nor does it sidestep confrontation of sin to avoid discomfort.

James describes godly wisdom as the alternative to the kind of so-called wisdom of the world:

For jealousy and selfishness are not God's kind of wisdom. Such things are earthly, unspiritual, inspired by the devil. For wherever there is jealousy or selfish ambition, there will be disorder and every kind of evil (James 3:15-16).

He had just warned his readers about the dangers of uncontrolled tongues: "If anyone can control his tongue, it proves he has perfect control over himself (James 3:2)." After expounding on the damage poisonous speech can do, he contrasts selfish worldly wisdom with unselfish godly wisdom. He then goes on to explain that relational conflicts come from selfish individualism: "What is causing the quarrels and fights among you? Isn't it because there is a whole army of evil desires within you (James 4:1)?" Worldly wisdom looks out for selfish interests at whatever cost to relationships. Godly wisdom seeks rich relationships at whatever cost to selfish interests.

It is crucial that Christians model godly wisdom in their business relationships.. Speaking the truth in love requires attention to the process as well as to the content of communication. As Paul says, "Although being a 'know-it-all' makes us feel important, what is really needed to build the church is love (I Corinthians 8:1)." Godly wisdom goes beyond knowing the truth to knowing how to live the truth, and how to explain the truth with such compassion that it will be received and applied by others. If the truth itself offends a person, we must not compromise for the sake of temporary comfort—only the truth can bring lasting peace. If anything about the way we communicate the truth is offensive, we must set aside our pride and find ways to speak it more lovingly.

The basic difference between godly wisdom and worldly wisdom is the contrast between faith and fear. The position of faith bases relationships on trust—trusting God frees us to trust each other. The position of fear bases relationships on distrust—looking out for self means distrusting others. Communication grounded in trust is upbeat, positive and productive. Communication grounded in distrust is suspicious, negative and self-protective. As James explains, problems in relationships stem from patterns of thought and speech which are characterized by fear rather than by faith. Shifting from a position of fear to a position of faith will revolutionize communication.

James 3 warns that what we say and how we say it can make the difference between blessing and disaster. Christ –like communication is truthful, peaceful, impartial, and straightforward. We will be respected by people to whom we have shown respect.

We are responsible for everything we say, and will be accountable for every idle word. Some talk too much and work too little; some are silent when encouraging words are needed. A wise man knows when to speak, what to say, and when to be silent. If you think yourself to be wiser than the other, be quiet about it. The quickest way to win an argument is to avoid it, if possible. If you must speak up, present your case through carefully chosen words and a logical, orderly presentation. Abe Lincoln once said, "The sin of silence, when protest is in order, makes cowards of men." As a rule people want praise, not flattery, and truth rather than false reassurance. It is an unusual person today who really listens, and is genuinely interested in what another has to say; yet businesses flourish where this trait is admired, taught, and respected. One secret of Wal-Mart's success was the value it placed on the customer; customers were always right, and returns were given without question. Saturday morning management meetings in Bentonville were "cheerleading" events, lavish with excitement and praise by the founder, Sam Walton, when he was at the helm.

Truthful, constructive words are essential to the work of God (Isaiah 55:11; II Peter 3:5-7). Jesus spoke life — giving words of eternal truth and power (Matthew 24:35; John 6:63, 68). If the work of God, as revealed in Christ, is being worked into our lives, our work will epitomize respectful, productive speech.

According to Proverbs:

• 16:23 *From a wise mind comes careful and persuasive speech.*

"My words shall fall upon you like the gentle rain and dew, like rain upon the tender grass, like showers on the hillside (Deuteronomy 32:1-2)." "Let your conversation be gracious as well as sensible, for then you will have the right answer for everyone (Colossians 4:6)." "Your conversation should be so sensible and logical that anyone who wants to argue will be ashamed of himself because there won't be anything to criticize in anything you say (Titus 2:8)!" When you are right, you can afford to be polite. Harsh words and high volume are signs of desperation which damage the credibility of any argument. People are most often convinced by the person who presents a case calmly and clearly.

"… How wonderful it is to be able to say the right thing at the right time (Proverbs 15:23)!" We have all suffered bouts of "foot-in-mouth disease," saying the wrong thing at the wrong time. "…The tongue is a small thing, but what enormous damage it can do (James 3:5)."There is no way to unsay damaging comments, but we can learn from our mistakes. Learning to think before we speak minimizes the risk of offense or misunderstanding. The person who speaks less may say more. Great wisdom can be expressed in few words, if they are carefully chosen.

• 16:24 *Kind words are like honey—enjoyable and healthful.*

"Timely advice is as lovely as golden apples in a silver basket (Proverbs 25:11)." "Everyone enjoys giving good advice, and how wonderful it is to be able to say the right thing at the right time!" A good man thinks before he speaks; the evil man pours out his evil words without a thought (Proverbs 15:28)." Weighing our words before we speak can save us from a ton of troubles. Finding the most comforting and productive thing to say, and saying it gently, calms the most troubled waters. A spoonful of medicine makes the fever go down, with or without sugar, and sweet common sense can take the heat out of confrontation.

- 19:22a *Kindness makes a man attractive.*

People thrive in the warmth and light of kindness. Goodwill and courtesy create lasting relationships, both personally and professionally. We want to have people around us who are encouraging and helpful. Bitterness is a strong repellent. Nobody likes a constant stream of cynicism.

- 15:4 *Gentle words cause life and health; griping brings discouragement.*

"A soft answer turns away wrath, but harsh words cause quarrels (Proverbs 15:1)." "A constant dripping on a rainy day and a cranky woman are much alike (Proverbs 27:15)!" Civility smooths conversation, helping people iron out their problems without burning each other. Perpetual criticism and complaining erodes the foundations of productive discussion.

- 14:23 *Work brings profit; talk brings poverty.*

"Don't talk so much. You keep putting your foot in your mouth. Be sensible and turn off the flow! When a good man speaks, he is worth listening to, but the words of fools are a dime a dozen (Proverbs 10:19-20)." Talk can be expensive, when there's work to be done. Friendly conversation and camaraderie are essential to human interaction, but running the mouth at idle kills productive cooperation. Any project can be buried in endless discussion.

- 20:19 *Don't tell your secrets to a gossip, unless you want them broadcast to the whole world.*

"Whatever they have said in the dark shall be heard in the light, and what you have whispered in the inner rooms shall be broadcast from the housetops for all to hear (Luke 12:3)!" "A gossip goes around spreading rumors, while a trustworthy man tries to quiet them (Proverbs 11:13)." Three people can keep a secret—if two of them are dead. We all like to be the first to tell each other the latest news. If the news is really sensational, we tend to exaggerate it even further. We don't let the facts ruin a good story. Gossip is the art of stretching the facts beyond the limits of credibility, and then making up fiction to fill in the gaps. Distortion of the truth turns molehills into mountains—or confidential comments into tabloid headlines.

- 30:10 *Never falsely accuse a man to his employer, lest he curse you for your sin.*

"Who art thou that judgest another man's servant? To his own master he standeth or falleth (Romans 14:4 KJV)." "Do not pass along untrue reports (Exodus 23:1)." Spreading rumors risks unintended consequences; making direct false accusations is an intentional attempt to harm another person. Trying to get an employee in trouble with his or her employer violates principles of personal integrity and professional ethics. It is never right to try to make oneself look good by making someone else look bad—yet cutthroat competitors do it every day.

Reports

Some people learn by others' mistakes; others are destined to make the same ones themselves. We can learn a lot about business by watching others' mistakes, and by reading about their successes and follies. Enron's failure was tragic, but it was made worse by lies, deceit, fraud, and greed. Reports to investors should always be accurate and understandable. When things are not going well, accurate reports and thoughtful explanations of new directions to be taken, or valid reasons for seeing things through and holding the course will be accepted, and confidence will be sustained. Truthfulness builds trust; lies and deceit will bring down any enterprise in time.

Clear, accurate, practical communication is essential to the work of God (Deuteronomy 29:29: Deuteronomy 30:11-14; Romans 10:8-9). Jesus brought a message from God (John 17:8, 14, 17); His followers continue His witness (John 17:20; I John 1:1-3; II Peter 1:16-19; I Corinthians 15:1-8). If the work of God, as revealed in Christ, is being worked into our lives, our work will epitomize truthful communication.

According to Proverbs:

- 15:30 *Pleasant sights and good reports give happiness and health.*
- 21:12 *The godly learn by watching ruin overtake the wicked.*
- 13:13 *The advice of a wise man refreshes like water from a mountain spring. Those accepting it become aware of the pitfalls ahead.*
- 18:13 *What a shame – yes, how stupid! – To decide before knowing the facts!*

"Finally, brethren, whatsoever things are true, whatsoever things are honest, whatsoever things are just, whatsoever things are pure, whatsoever things are lovely, whatsoever things are of good report; if there be any virtue, and if there be any praise, think on these things (Philippians 4:8 KJV)." We can never learn everything, but we can learn from everybody. All kinds of valuable lessons can be learned in all kinds of ways. Seeing and hearing good things can inspire us to good thoughts and actions. We can learn by observing the good and bad experiences of others, and trying to avoid their mistakes. Good advice from knowledgeable people can teach us to prepare for potential problems. Careful research gives us confidence that we know what we need to know in order to do what we want to do.

- 18:15 *The intelligent man is always open to new ideas. In fact, he looks for them.*
- 9:9 *Teach a wise man, and he will be the wiser: teach a good man, and he will learn more.*

• 12:1a *To learn, you must want to be taught.*

"Learn to be wise," he said, "and develop good judgment and common sense! I cannot over-emphasize this point." Cling to wisdom – she will protect you. Love her – she will guard you (Proverbs 1:5-6)." "If you want to know what God wants you to do, ask him, and he will gladly tell you, for he is always ready to give a bountiful supply of wisdom to all who ask him; he will not resent it (James 1:5)." What we don't know might hurt us — our unjustified assumptions can ruin us. Wisdom takes nothing for granted, questioning even the most obvious answers. For most of us, changing our minds takes sharp confrontation, candid intervention — or an act of God. If we are wise, gentler prodding will move us to re-think our pet theories. We may even learn the art of confronting ourselves, and intervening in our own delusional thinking. Only a fool persists in fooling himself.

• 21:11a *The wise man learns by listening.*

"He that answereth a matter before he heareth it, it is folly and shame unto him (Proverbs 18:13 KJV)." "Dear brothers, don't ever forget that it is best to listen much, speak little, and not become angry … (James 1:19)." There are more than two sides to every story. Wisdom includes good judgment in assessing problems, and creativity in proposing solutions. Good judgment requires patience and fairness — hearing and weighing the facts. Creativity requires divergent thinking — finding novel ways to connect seemingly unrelated ideas. Good judgment and creativity are seldom perfectly balanced in a single personality. Those who have learned to color inside the lines find it difficult to think outside the box, and those with free-ranging minds have a hard time reining in their enthusiasm. We need the counterbalance of people whose personalities and perspectives are different from our own. We need to listen until the differences come together in a more productive solution than we could have found on our own.

• 15:14 *A wise man is hungry for truth, while the mocker feeds on trash.*

"Buy the truth, and sell it not; also wisdom, and instruction, and understanding (Proverbs 23:23 KJV)." "Dear friends, remember what the apostles of our Lord Jesus Christ told you, that in the last times there would come these scoffers, whose sole purpose in life is to enjoy themselves in every evil way imaginable (Jude 1:19)." "I will set no wicked thing before mine eyes: I hate the work of them that turn aside; it shall not cleave to me (Psalm 101:3 KJV)" Focusing on the truth fills a person with God's wisdom; focusing on trivia fills a person with the world's foolishness. Whatever we're full of spills out when we're bumped. Those who feed on God's word grow and prosper—those who fill their minds with trash will shrivel and die, spiritually.

• 13:17 *An unreliable messenger can cause a lot of trouble. Reliable communication permits progress.*

"You must give them my messages whether they listen or not... (Ezekiel 2:7)." "Didn't I tell your messengers that even if you gave me a palace filled with silver and gold, I could not go beyond the word of Jehovah, and could not say a word of my own? I said that I would say only what Jehovah says (Numbers 24:12-13!" "You tolerate some among you who do as Balaam did when he taught Balak how to ruin the people of Israel... Revelation 2:14)." God's commission to His messengers is a good model for accurate communication. They were to deliver the message clearly and completely, without altering it to please their hearers. Neither fear of rejection nor hope of reward will affect a faithful messenger's delivery of a fateful message. Even Balaam limited his prophecy to the message God gave him— but then, for the sake of Balak's gifts, he added suggestions which temporarily subverted the prophecy. Clear, accurate communication facilitates productive action—a self-seeking messenger misrepresents the one who sent him, and sabotages his employer's intentions.

Moses' Meekness

Do nice guys always finish last? Not in God's book. According to Jesus, the meek shall inherit the earth (Matthew 5:5). Who are the meek? Well, Moses was one of them, in fact a prime example: "Now the man Moses was very meek, above all the men which were upon the face of the earth (Numbers 12:3 KJV)." What is meekness? Different Bible translations link meekness to humility, poverty of spirit, and submissiveness. That may sound like a definition of a human doormat, somebody who lets everybody walk all over him. But Paul tells us, "Be honest in your estimate of yourselves, measuring your value by how much faith God has given you (Romans 12:3)." Humility is making no pretense to be anything more or less than you really are in God's sight. Poverty of spirit is recognizing your dependence on God. Submissiveness to God is often rebellion against the world. Meekness is not weakness—it is strength under control.

Moses was humble enough to recognize his own limitations. When God chose Him as His spokesman, Moses argued that he lacked the eloquence to speak before Pharaoh. Ironically, he dared to debate with God about his inability to argue God's case in front of a mere human being. Godly meekness finds its strength in such freedom in communicating with God—bold prayer precedes and accompanies great works of God in the world. God gave Moses two ways to get beyond his perceived speech problem: his brother Aaron would do most of the talking, and his rod would be used to teach object lessons, miracles showing God's power over the so-called gods of the Egyptians. Moses could speak softly, and carry a big stick. (Exodus 3-4:17)

Moses might have learned poverty of spirit the hard way. To his credit, he gave up his privileged place in the royal family of Egypt, and accepted identification as a member of a slave race. Josephus, the historian, tells stories of the brilliant military career Moses had as a leader of the Egyptians. This is quite possible, and, if true, adds dimensions to the picture of his leadership. In any event, Moses never lost his connection to God's people, the oppressed Israelites. On one of his visits to the slave camp, he killed an Egyptian who was beating an Israelite. Moses thought his people would recognize him as their deliverer, but instead, one of them said, "Who made you a ruler and judge over us? Acts 7:23-27)." The Israelites considered Moses a traitor, and the Egyptians branded him a murderer. Moses ran, fleeing the country. Moses had tried to lift himself up, but God knocked him down, and he landed on the backside of the desert. (Exodus 2:1-15).

Moses became submissive to God through years of hard work in obscurity. His humiliation brought him down from the royal court of Egypt to a shepherd's tent in the desert. God spoke to Balaam through a donkey; He spoke to Moses through shrubbery. Yet, even as God's voice came from a bush, Moses thought God could not speak through him. But he knew better than to argue endlessly with God. He packed up his family, and headed back to Egypt. (Exodus 4:18-31).

The rest is history. God used Moses mightily to bring the Israelites out of Egypt, and to mold their national identity. The meekest man on earth became the deliverer, the nation-builder, of the most enduring people-group on earth. Recognizing his own limitations, giving up his pride, and submitting to God, Moses succeeded in a seemingly impossible enterprise. Can we follow his example?

Consequences

What we get demonstrates the quality of what we do.

What we do with what we get demonstrates the quality of who we are.

While the adversities and limitations of life in a sin-tainted world affect all of us, people of godly character who conduct themselves wisely will live effectively. Following biblical principles will bring positive results in every area of life. How we handle the rewards and successes we earn is a joyful responsibility.

What we get

Financial Reward

"The laborer is worthy of his reward" (I Timothy 5:18b). Planning, hard work, and good human relations will bring good results. Being in the path of God's blessing brings spiritual blessing, but we can also expect to be paid fairly by those we serve well, and to receive good returns from wise investments.

Everyone likes to be rewarded for conscientious effort. A fair wage for hard work is a natural expectation. Whom we trust for our reward should be our primary concern. How we earn the reward will be our legacy to future generations. What we do with the reward is both ministry and testimony. In all our business dealings, from start to finish, we need to keep our focus on the Lord as we work diligently and purposefully.

Life is not always fair, but God is (Deuteronomy 5:9-10; 32:4). Jesus promises both temporal and eternal blessings to those who commit their lives to Him (Mark 10:29-30). If our lives are lived in conformity to God's character and work, we can expect His blessing. While health and wealth are not guaranteed, it is reasonable to believe that the way God prescribes is the only way to secure success.

According to Proverbs:

- 11:31 *Even the godly shall be rewarded here on earth; how much more the wicked!*

"... For he [God] gives his sunlight to both the evil and the good, and sends rain on the just and on the unjust too (Matthew 5:45)." "... a man will always reap just the kind of crop he sows (Galatians 6:7)!" "Yes, they go out weeping, carrying seed for sowing, and return singing, carrying their sheaves (Psalm 126:6)." "He [God] searches all hearts and examines deepest motives so he can give to each person his right reward, according to his deeds—how he has lived (Jeremiah 17:10)." Work brings its fair consequences. Material benefits come to those who seek them through hard work; spiritual benefits come to those who seek to please God through obedient faith.

- 11:28 *Trust in your money and down you go! Trust in God and flourish as a tree!*

"They trust in their wealth and boast about how rich they are, yet not one of them, though rich as kings, can ransom his own brother from the penalty of sin (Psalm 49:6-7)!" "Tell those who are rich not to be proud and not to trust in their money, which will soon be gone, but their pride and trust should be in the living God who always richly gives us all we need for our enjoyment (I Timothy 6:17)." No matter how rich a person gets, somebody else may have more houses, a bigger boat, and a more exotic car. The third-richest person in town may know less about contentment than the third-poorest. Riches are uncertain—fortune can turn to misfortune overnight. Rock solid investments can turn to quicksand. People who take pride in the empires they have built for themselves risk the hard lessons of God's judgment. (Daniel 4:27-33).

Financial rewards for honest work are more satisfying and secure than wealth gained through deceit and manipulation. God is present and active in the lives of those who respond to Him in obedient faith. Peace and contentment cannot be bought with uncertain riches, but are freely given to those who trust God completely

• 28:22 *Trying to get rich quick is evil and leads to poverty.*

"But they that will be rich fall into temptation and a snare, and into many foolish and hurtful lusts, which drown men in destruction and perdition. For the love of money is the root of all evil: which while some coveted after, they have erred from the faith, and pierced themselves through with many sorrows (I Timothy 6:9-10 KJV)." An obsession with getting and spending money drains life of its meaning. Like those who are famous for being famous, those who are rich for the sake of riches may be envied, but not admired. The pursuit of wealth is their all-consuming passion which erodes their character, taints their relationships with other people, and obliterates their interest in God.

• 4:18 *But the good man walks along in the ever brightening light of God's favor....*

• 10:16a *A good man's earnings advance the cause of righteousness.*

• 10:24b *A good man's hopes all come true.*

"Be delighted with the Lord. Then he will give you all your heart's desires.... The steps of good men are directed by the Lord. He delights in each step they take (Psalm 37:4, 23)." "... They delight in doing everything God wants them to.... All they do shall prosper (Psalm 1:2, 3)." "Honor the Lord by giving Him the first part of all your income, and He will fill your barns with wheat and barley and overflow your wine vats with the finest wines (Proverbs 3:9-10)." "But seek ye first the kingdom of God, and his righteousness; and all these things shall be added unto you (Matthew 6:33 KJV)." When God's people focus on God's glory, they want what He wants, and He abundantly supplies their needs. Investing our lives and our fortunes in the cause of God's righteousness brings assurance that God will bless us. We enjoy His presence and activity in our lives as we draw close to Him in obedient faith.

Financial rewards are secured by integrity. What has been called "the protestant ethic" is simply biblical wisdom applied to common sense economic reality. Work conscientiously, and you will be rewarded fairly. Spend conservatively, and you will not plunge into debt. Save consistently, and your wealth will grow. Give cheerfully, and you will glorify God by helping others.

- 20:21-22 *If your enemy is hungry, give him food! If he is thirsty, give him something to drink! This will make him feel ashamed of himself, and God will reward you.*

- 28:10 *A curse on those who lead the godly astray. But men who encourage the upright to do good shall be given a worthwhile reward.*

"... Whenever we can we should always be kind to everyone, and especially to our Christian brothers (Galatians 6:10)." "Tell [those who are rich] to use their money to do good. They should be rich in good works and should give happily to those in need (I Timothy 6:18)." "Don't forget to do good and to share what you have with those in need, for such sacrifices are very pleasing to him (Hebrews 13:16)." "Remember, too, that knowing what is right to do and then not doing it is sin (James 4:17)." We are blessed in order to bless others. Mercy and kindness are essential to God's character, and should be evident in the character of His people. Love for one another is the mark of true followers of Christ—generosity to everyone proves that we fully trust Him to supply all our needs.

Financial rewards are sanctified by generosity. "Share the wealth" is not merely a slogan of socialism; it is an attitude rooted in biblical wisdom. God's people are blessed in order to bless others. There is no Marxist communism in Acts 4, simply voluntary sacrifice to meet real needs: "...no one felt that what he owned was his own; everyone was sharing (Acts 4:32)." Local churches tend to become homogenized—they identify with the socio-economic level of their leading members. Leaders should remember that the first church officers were chosen to distribute food to the poorest members (Acts 6:1-6). Every individual child of God should be looking for opportunities to do good to someone who has less. Our corporate ministry should provide encouragement and example in recognizing and meeting material, as well as spiritual needs.

- 13:22 *When a good man dies, he leaves an inheritance to his grandchildren; but when a sinner dies, his wealth is stored up for the godly.*
- 28:8 *Income from exploiting the poor will end up in the hands of someone who pities them.*

"... Keep and seek for all the commandments of the LORD your God: that ye may possess this good land, and leave it for an inheritance for your children after you for ever (I Chronicles 28:8 KJV)." "Their inward thought is, that their houses shall continue for ever, and their dwelling places to all generations; they call their lands after their own names. Nevertheless man being in honor abideth not: he is like the beasts that perish (Psalm 49:11-12 KJV)." "Look here, you rich men, now is the time to cry and groan with anguished grief because of all the terrible troubles ahead of you…. That is what you have stored up for yourselves, to receive on that coming day of judgment (James 5:1-3)." Obedient faith brings God's blessing. Obsession with ill-gotten wealth brings God's judgment.

Lasting Success

"The great and indispensable help to success is character. Character is crystallized habit, the result of training and conviction in the affairs of life or of business," says Burton in *The Anatomy of Melancholy*.

Treating your employees right puts you on the pathway to success. Love Box Company has a private school teaching classical education that is available at their plant for their worker's children. They also provide a gym for their employees to ensure good health and to lower work-related injuries. They offer periodic self – defense clinics for their female employees, a service which may have saved the life of an employee who was able to defend herself against three attackers. The company pays well, and provides a future for its workers. Is it any wonder that many workers retire after more then 30 years of service?

Boaz, whose character shines throughout the book of Ruth, had a similar respect for people around him, and it paid off for both him, and his workers. In your mind's eye, see him exchange greetings as he passes by his fields. The gleaners cry out, "Sir, the Lord bless you!" Boaz replies, "The Lord bless you as well." We are never lifted up by putting others down; a family, a church, or a business is built up as all its members are built up.

The following proverbs show the balance between faith and works in success. The health of your business also depends on these important principles.

According to Proverbs:

- 3:1-6 *My son, never forget the things I've taught you. If you want a long and satisfying life, closely follow my instructions. Never forget to be truthful and kind. Hold these virtues tightly. Write them deep within your heart. If you want favor with both God and man, and a reputation for good judgment and common sense, then trust in the Lord completely; don't ever trust yourself. In everything you do, put God first, and He will direct you and crown your efforts with success.*

Faithful obedience is they key to a productive, rewarding life—we must be willing to do what God says we should do." But seek ye first the kingdom of God, and his righteousness; and all these things shall be added unto you (Matthew 6:33 KJV)." Strange as it sounds to business school graduates, obedient faith is the key to ultimate success. Fear of the Lord, godly wisdom, and proven character build a solid, productive life. God created and owns everything, and he put us on earth as caretakers and distributors of His wealth. He knows our needs, and freely supplies them as we conform to His character and carry out His plans. In a faith-based approach to business ethics, faith comes before ethics, and ethics come before business. A business-based approach to ethics and faith reverses God's priorities.

- 16:3   *Commit your way to the Lord, then it will succeed.*

    Obedient faith is the foundation of true success — we must be confident that God will do what He says He will do.

- 22:4   *True humility and respect for the Lord lead a man to riches, honor, and a long life.*

    Seeking God's glory rather than our own is the path of God's blessing.

- 15:22   *Plans go wrong with too few counselors; many counselors bring success.*

    The first step towards success is careful, well-advised planning. Dreams must be formed into plans before they can become reality.

- 22:29   *Do you know a hard working man? He shall be successful and stand before kings!*

    Planning is effective only when it is followed by hard work to carry out the plan.

- 28:13   *A man who refuses to admit his mistakes can never be successful. But if he confesses and forsakes them, he gets another chance.*

    No matter how carefully we plan, or how hard we work, course corrections may be necessary.

- 28:12a *When the godly are successful, everyone is glad…*

    When we seek God's glory through careful planning, hard work, and response to correction, God blesses everyone involved in our efforts.

Abraham's Affluence

Abraham was a man of faith, an example of all who simply believe what God says, and act on that belief (Romans 4; Hebrews 11:8-12). In his original home, his family "served other gods (Joshua 24:2)," which may mean that they had household idols in addition to recognition of the one true God, or that they engaged in outright paganism. Josephus cited evidence that Abraham was proficient in worship of the heavenly bodies, but that he became unpopular when he became a strong advocate of monotheism (Josephus, *Antiquities of the Jews*, Book 1, Chapter 7, sections 1 and 2). Of course, Josephus had a vested interest in making Abraham a hero. When the biblical account picks up the story, it simply says that God said, "Go!" and Abraham went (Genesis 12:1-4).

That is the essence of obedient faith—what God says, we do. Like Paul on the Damascus road, Abraham may have been surprised to hear from God so directly, and his plans and preconceived notions may have been disrupted, but his response was decisive. When God speaks, people need to listen.

God didn't just dictate orders to Abraham; He made promises. Abraham's faith would be rewarded with rich blessings. Material prosperity was only one aspect of the blessing. Abraham's descendants would form whole nations, and inhabit productive land. The whole world would benefit from the fruits of Abraham's faith. (Genesis 12:1-3).

Abraham's material prosperity increased throughout his lifetime, but so did his faith. Whether through good management, good treatment of employees, or the goodwill of others, Abraham got richer and richer. Good things flowed his way—"affluence" means, "flowing towards." Yet, when he and his nephew faced conflict over keeping their huge flocks, Abraham said, "You choose where you want to settle—I'll take whatever is left." (Genesis 13). When he brought his three hundred eighteen servants back in victory from a battle, he refused a personal reward: "I don't want anybody but God to be able to say he made me rich." (Genesis 14).

Do what God says, accept what God gives, and give God all the glory. That was the secret of Abraham's affluence. If we can live that way, we can find real contentment—the place of blessing is the place of obedient faith.

Did Abraham get everything God promised? Not exactly, at least not in his lifetime on earth. He lived as a nomad in the Promised Land, and the only real estate he owned at his death was a cemetery plot. (Hebrews 11:9-10; Acts 7:5; Genesis 25:7-10). There's a lesson in that, too—the only permanent possession we can have on earth is a grave.

Abraham trusted that God would keep His promises, even if Abraham died before they were fulfilled. As they say when a billionaire dies, "How much did he leave?" "All of it." In Abraham's case, as for all people of true faith, material wealth is not the only blessing which flows from God's promises.

What we do with what we get

Stewardship

From start to finish, our attitude towards business affairs must be biblical. "Godliness with contentment is great gain;" selfish desire for riches can ruin a person's life (James 6:6-11). If our primary focus is to advance God's purposes, He will "tend to business" concerning our material needs (Matthew 6:33).

Being considered a good steward is the highest compliment a Christian can be given. Only God knows whether we are doing our best in this area. The fastest doesn't always win the race (Asahel) or the strongest the battle (David and Goliath). It isn't the size of the dog that is in the fight it is the size of the fight that is in the dog that wins.

People today tend to waste a lot of time, energy, and materials. One man told me (and he was extremely proud of the fact) that he traveled to Japan to buy his shirts. He only paid $200.00 per shirt there, while his peers were paying $350.00 a shirt and more! Some builders leave their tools out in the weather, and painters won't even clean their brushes or rollers. They claim it is cheaper to replace them than to clean them! When a workman does not take pride in his tools, his workmanship will lack the perfection his profession should require.

I knew a man who got rich by pulling out railroad tracks. He was paid for his work by the railroad, and then he sold the rail for scrap metal and the ties to landscape architects. Another man I met, whose business fed one-third of the nation's cattle, baled tumble weeds, corn stock, and other edible materials people were throwing away, and kept the protein content two points higher than he was contracted to do. These men were literally getting rich on things others were discarding!

While traveling through Scotland by train, I engaged in conversation with a man who was an author of novels. He had written two bestsellers! The remarkable thing was that he always wrote while on a train. He had developed this strange habit because he wrote his first bestseller during two-hour-a-day train rides while commuting to and from a factory job. He grew so accustomed to writing while riding that he now rides whenever he is writing a new novel. He had transformed a lengthy commuter ride into profitable work time; while others were napping, he built a new career for himself.

I once counseled with a young woman who was date-raped on her first date at age sixteen. She made the choice to keep her baby but was very concerned about her future because of the demands of motherhood. Her parents agreed to help her with babysitting while she continued living with them and going to college. Her goal was to become an engineer. She began to think of ways she could pay for her college as well as take care of the needs of her child. She began using her parents' garage to sew designs on old Levi's. That home-based business brought in $70,000 in its first year of operation, which was more than her father made that year! She now has a Ph.D. in engineering, as does her husband, and continues to run the business now from her own location, employing five people.

I know two women who are both wealthy; both invest in the stock market. One has gone to every seminar and class she can find to increase her knowledge of market trends and investment strategies; the other has relied on an investment firm alone for her security. One has made wise decisions and watches the market daily; the other spends her time doing what she wants to do. One has done extremely well and the other has lost more money than most of us will ever make. Can you guess which one is doing well?

According to Proverbs:

• 27:24   *…So watch your business interest closely. Know the state of your flocks and herds.*

"But don't begin until you count the cost. For who would begin construction of a building without first getting estimates and then checking to see if he has enough money to pay the bills? (Luke 15:28)." "Develop your business first before building your house (Proverbs 24:27)." Being a good steward of what you have starts with a clear understanding of what you have have. Careful analysis of assets should precede any major expenditure. Although loans and credit make it easy to spend money you don't have, they can lead to disaster if you're betting on expected income which you never get. Making sure your assets balance your debts provides a sure foundation for building your business. You have to make a living before you develop a lifestyle.

• 24:30-31   *I walked by the field of a certain lazy fellow and saw that it was overgrown with thorns, and covered with weeds; and its walls were broken down.*

"An empty stable stays clean – but there is no income from an empty stable (Proverbs 14:4)." Good stewardship includes gathering the equipment and putting forth the effort to reach worthy goals. Whatever the enterprise, you'll need the right tools and the right materials, and you'll need to work hard to succeed.

• 12:27   *A lazy man won't even dress the game he gets while hunting, but the diligent man makes good use of everything he finds.*

"Some men are so lazy they won't even feed themselves (Proverbs 19:24)!" "He is too tired even to lift his food from his dish to his mouth (Proverbs 26:15)!" A good steward is not wasteful, but wisely uses every available resource. If you're

109

waiting for the good things in life to be served to you on a silver platter, you'd better buy some paper plates.

• 17:16 *It is senseless to pay tuition to educate a rebel who has no heart for the truth.*

"You can't separate a rebel from his foolishness though you crush him to powder (Proverbs 27:22)." Good stewardship includes a candid assessment of one's own knowledge and skills—knowing one's limitations makes a person ready to learn.

• 10:27a *Reverence for God adds hours to each day.*

"Teach a wise man, and he will be the wiser; teach a good man, and he will learn more; for the reverence and fear of God are basic to all wisdom. Knowing God results in every other kind of understanding. I, Wisdom, will make the hours of your day more profitable and the years of your life more fruitful (Proverbs 9:9-11)." "So teach us to number our days, that we may apply our hearts unto wisdom (Psalm 90:12 KJV)."

Good stewardship means making the best use of time, as well as of other resources. Working hard brings desired results—working smart brings them sooner.

Giving

Keeping up with the Joneses takes on a whole new meaning in Northwest Arkansas. The late Mrs. Bernice Jones, of the Jones Trucking Lines, after the sale of the business, began a campaign to give her money away. A wonderful Christian lady, she began by building a fitness center complete with an ice rink, Olympic-size swimming pool, first class gym, basketball court, indoor running track, weight training room, meeting rooms for anniversary celebrations and wedding receptions, computer rooms, and a theater with free Cokes and pop corn. Even the ice skates are loaned out at no cost. I could write a book about all she did, including building first class elementary schools in poor areas that would rival most junior colleges, and putting computers in every classroom of every school in Springdale,

Arkansas! Even after her accountant reportedly stole 93 million dollars, she was able to complete her mission before dying at 100 years of age!

The "chicken man", Don Tyson, and family, owners of Tyson, Inc., have built Little League fields and soccer fields complete with batting cages, in a complex that is truly magnificent. It is impossible to drive by the Tyson Complex without seeing kids (and sometimes "big" kids) playing on these fields. It is a model for others to follow. Those people truly know how to invest in our youth.

Some people have the idea that we get to consume upon ourselves. "Get what you can, can what you get, and get it while you can still spend it," seems to be their motto. As if life was all about themselves! The Scriptures teach another story. We are not owners of things, nor do we receive them independently, apart from a kind Providence. God gives us stewardship over His wealth. With that stewardship come certain responsibilities and management expectations. The Scriptures state in Luke 12:48, "To whom much is given, of him much shall be required." This is true in the areas of natural gifts ("for what do you have that you have not received," I Corinthians 4:7) and it is true in the realm of spiritual gifts ("He gives severally to every person as He wills," I Corinthians 12:11). It is also true of wealth (The Parable of the Talents—Luke 12).

The Lord is very concerned with how we handle the wealth He entrusts to us. We don't give to get, as some wolves in sheep's clothing would have us believe; the so-called, "name it and claim it" crowd. We give to show that we understand ownership. God owns it all. We acknowledge that principle by doing what He says in returning a portion for His direct use in feeding the poor, in tithing to the church, or wherever else He may direct us to give His substance. Understanding giving puts everything material in perspective; everything is to glorify God. Does God supply all our needs? Yes (Philippians 4:19), because of His good pleasure and watch-care over us (Ephesians 1:9). Unfortunately, as the great evangelist, D.L. Moody, once remarked, "The pocketbook seems to be the last thing to be converted."

Follow the truths of Scripture in your business, and you will be blessed to bless others.

According to Proverbs:

• 3:9,10 *Honor the Lord by giving Him the first part of all your income, and He will fill your barns with wheat and barley and overflow your wine vats with the finest wines.*

"On every Lord's Day each of you should put aside something from what you have earned during the week, and use it for [an] offering (I Corinthians 16:2)." "Bring all the tithes into the storehouse…; if you do, I will open up the windows of heaven for you and pour out a blessing so great you won't have room to take it in (Malachi 3:10)!" A commitment to systematic, proportional giving is an act of obedient faith which puts a person in a position to receive God's richest blessings. Our giving displays God's own generosity; He is honored when our character reflects His character.

• 11:24, 25 *It is possible to give away and become richer! It is also possible to hold on too tightly and lose everything. Yes, the liberal man shall be rich! By watering others, he waters himself.*

"And how does a man benefit if he gains the whole world and loses his soul in the process (Mark 8:36)?" "Give generously, for your gifts will return to you later. Divide your gifts among many, for in the days ahead you yourself may need help (Ecclesiastes 11:1-3)." "For the man who uses well what he has been given shall be given more, and he shall have abundance. But from the man who is unfaithful, even what he has shall be taken from him (Matthew 25:29)." Giving enriches character, wins respect and trust, and builds a foundation for continuing success. We are blessed to be a blessing to others.

- 21:25-26 *The lazy man longs for many things but his hands refuse to work. He is greedy to get, while the godly love to give.*

"Thou shalt not covet ... (Exodus 20:17)." "He who does not work shall not eat (II Thessalonians 3:10)." Covetousness and laziness are a destructive combination. Desperately wanting what we are not wiling to work for creates a multitude of sins. A lazy person seeks wealth and comfort not through work, but through deceiving or coercing others

- 19:17 *When you help the poor you are lending to the Lord—and He pays wonderful interest on your loan!*
- 21:13 *He who shuts his ears to the cries of the poor will be ignored in his own time of need.*
- 14:21 *To despise the poor is to sin. Blessed are those who pity them.*
- 14:31 *Anyone who oppresses the poor is insulting God who made them. To help the poor is to honor God.*
- 15:25 *The LORD destroys the possessions of the proud; but cares for widows.*
- 21:3 *God is more pleased when we are just and fair than when we give Him gifts.*
- 28:27 *If you give to the poor, your needs will be supplied! But a curse upon those who close their eyes to poverty.*
- 22:9 *Happy is the generous man, the one who feeds the poor.*

Against the advice of friends, I made a no-interest loan to a family who were about to lose their home. My friends had tried to help them in various ways in the past, and thought the loan was a bad idea: it seemed unlikely that they would pay the loan back. I have always had faith in God's people, but I also have a reasonable expectation of failure. I also know that as believers in Christ we are to help the poor—and they were definitely poor.

Many people have the idea that the best predictor of future behavior is past behavior. If I believed that, I would be forced to believe that there would be no hope for any of us. Churchill once said, "If your past quarrels with your present there is no future." For us believers, all life is present and future as we disregard the past and press forward to a glorious future. (Philippians 3:13). So I made the loan.

Several times during the next year the couple attempted to establish a payment plan. They wrote and told me of their intentions, and what I could expect. I always replied cordially, but without great expectations, as the man's job situation was always tenuous in the hard economics of the building trade he was in. Sure enough, one payment was made, and then there was a long gap, and another letter sent with an apology and another plan. This happened on three separate occasions over the course of a year or two. Then in the middle of very tough times, after the bubble burst in the housing market, a check arrived for the full amount. The check was accompanied by a nice thank-you note, and an invitation for coffee, fellowship and rejoicing over God's provision of a stable job at a time when many couples were receiving unemployment notices. The couple and their sweet kids kept their home, received a great job, and paid their no-interest loan back. I wasn't the only help they had received; another couple from their church Bible study gave them a gift, freely given, and asking for nothing in return. This couple had a real need; interest-free loans are known and expected in the bible as well as gifts with no expectation of returns. (Leviticus 19:9-10; 25:35-37, Isaiah 58:6-12)

Do acts compassion and generosity always turn out with a happy ending? No, of course not. Don't give expecting a return; give to the poor because it is the right thing to do. Loan money with little expectation of a return, and see the blessing of God on your life and in the lives of others. Jesus said," it is better to give than to receive" (Acts 20:35). He was either lying or telling the truth! (Numbers 23:17)

Investments

There are about as many investment strategies as there are people. Most are based on greed and fear: desiring to amass wealth for oneself, worrying that it might be lost to others. I know of a man who entrusted a young man with his retirement savings. At first the young man was given a small amount, and won great wealth through investments. The man seeing the return gave everything to the young man, and he lost it all. Wealth never satisfies the longing of the soul-wealth for wealth's sake is a trap and a folly. Solomon tells us in that, "He that loveth silver shall not be satisfied with silver, nor he that loveth abundance, with increase; this is also a waste" (Ecclesiastes 5:10).

During premarital counseling, I spent a long time with a young man who asked a lot of financial and investment questions. I explained my philosophy of investing in eight areas which I drew from Ecclesiastes 11:2. I explained that it is easy to keep up with eight areas. In less than a half hour each day a person can follow their progress, research companies they invest in, analyze market trends, and make adjustments when necessary. This simple investment plan allows people to work their regular jobs and take care of family responsibilities.

I followed up on our conversation a few months after the wedding. The young man said he was advised to let a professional invest the couple's money and not mess with it themselves. I knew the man he was advised to use, nice person, but hardly deserving the confidence this young man was placing in him. I am not against professionals (one of the companies I suggested he place one of his eight investments in was Vanguard) but, I was amazed in how easily he had suddenly placed his total financial faith in professionals.

Have faith in God, watch your investments closely, says wise Solomon (Proverbs 27:23).

According to Proverbs:

- 11:31 *Even the godly shall be rewarded here on earth; how much more the wicked!*

"Wherever your treasure is, there your heart and thoughts will also be (Luke 12:34)." "Be not deceived; God is not mocked: for whatsoever a man soweth, that shall he also reap (Galatians 6:7 KJV)."

- 28:20 *The man who wants to do right will get a rich reward. But the man who wants to get rich quick will quickly fail.*
- 11:18 *The evil man gets rich for the moment, but the good man's reward lasts forever.*
- 13:11 *Wealth from gambling quickly disappears; wealth from hard work grows.*
- 28:22 *Trying to get rich quick is evil and leads to poverty.*
- 11:28 *Trust in your money and down you go! Trust in God and flourish as a tree!*
- 10:2-3 *Ill-gotten gain brings no lasting happiness; right living does. The Lord will not let a good man starve to death, nor will He let the wicked man's riches continue forever.*

You cannot be mastered by money and by God at the same time (Luke 16:13), but you can serve God with your money (Luke 18:22). The secret of biblical wealth lies in the principle of ownership. God owns it all—we are only poor stewards of his riches, investing for eternal purposes. We must seek His kingdom first, rather than our own prosperity (Matthew 6:33). True disciples of Jesus do not cling to possessions, but forsake their hold. This is not just a willingness to forsake (where your heart is there your treasure is also), but a true forsaking (Luke 14:33).We sell all and buy the Pearl of great price. We feed the poor. We help the needy. We help the orphan. We help the widow. Remember, "He that is faithful in little is faithful in much" (Luke 16:10).

According to Proverbs:

- 10:22 *The Lord's blessing is our greatest wealth. All our work adds nothing to it.*

- 2:6-9 *For the Lord grants wisdom! His every word is a treasure of knowledge and understanding. He grants good sense to the godly-His saints. He is their shield, protecting them and guarding their pathway. He shows how to distinguish right from wrong, how to find the right decision every time.*

- 3:4-6 *If you want favor with both God and man, and a reputations for good judgment and common sense, then trust the Lord completely; don't ever trust yourself. In everything you do, put God first, and He will direct you and crown your efforts with success.*

- 28:8 *Income from exploiting the poor will end up in the hands of someone who pities them.*

- 28:12 *When the godly are successful, everyone is glad. When the wicked succeed, everyone is sad.*

The Bible has much to say on the subject of investments. One of the signs of the last days is that people will spend their money on temporary self-promotion and pleasure, collecting more and more for the dump (Job 21:13). God gives us all something to invest for eternity: gifts, talents, accomplishments, personalities. Whatever He gives we invest in the kingdom. If he gives substance, we minister substance (Luke 8:3). . Our motivation for investing is to escape from a meaningless existence. A good man's reward lasts forever (Proverbs 11:18). Why? Because he invests in eternal things. We don't trust in what we invest in, we trust in God (Proverbs 11:28). We realize that our greatest blessing is spiritual (Ephesians 1:3 and Proverbs 10:22).

Jim Beckman, M.D. is as content on a tractor as he is behind a scalpel doing plastic surgery. He and his wife, Charlie, are avid duck and turkey hunters and generally the best folks to hang out with you can find in Arkansas. Jim and Charlie have been involved in missions for many years and he was one of the first plastic surgeons on the ground in Iraq helping people that were part of our collateral damage.

Their company, Therapon, Inc., a cosmetic company, is what Jim calls a "kingdom company" and is positioned to give 51% of their profits to missions and Christian concerns.

What is your plan to build God's kingdom?

According to Proverbs:

- 10:16   *The good man's earnings advance the cause of righteousness. The evil man squanders his on sin.*

- 10:28   *The hope of good men is eternal happiness; the hopes of evil men are all in vain. God protects the upright but destroys the wicked. 30 The good shall never lose God's blessings, but the wicked shall lose everything.*

- 11:4   *Your riches won't help you on Judgment Day; only righteousness counts then.*

- 11:24-26   *It is possible to give away and become richer! It is also possible to hold on too tightly and lose everything. Yes, the liberal man shall be rich! By watering others, he waters himself. People curse the man who holds his grain for higher prices, but they bless the man who sells it to them in their time of need.*

We receive money to invest from several sources. You have heard it said, "IT TAKES MONEY TO MAKE MONEY". After you have done careful research of the principles the Bible reveals, you need capital before you dare to invest. Start with your stuff. If you haven't used an item in a year, sell it! That is capital! Now you have something to start with. Next, stop spending God's money! That's more capital to invest. Next, cut down on your payments. This is simply common sense, grandmother-talk. Make it fun, look at last year's utilities bills for each month, and try as an individual, a couple or a family to shave off amounts. Put up notes like." God made light conserve it" "Turn Off the switch. Cold Air Is Not FREE" "Be Ye

Warmed—Put On A Sweater", etc. You now have more capital to invest. A friend of mine has an "eat like a third world country" day—rice and milk. What you save in food that day, invest for more capital. Stop your special coffee latte and muffin, and have as much as an extra $150.00 a month worth of capital. Ride-share, walk to work, ride a bike to work three days a week .Capital, capital, capital! Good stewardship of God's money equals more money to be a steward of. You are wise; think of ways to apply these principles. Most financial counselors will tell you to have about five or six months of liquid assets on hand before investing (That may be where Peter fell short in the tax mess that the Lord pulled him out of). God does look after the Godly, but that is not an excuse to be sloppy.

According to Proverbs:

- 21:20 *The wise man saves for the future, but the foolish man spends whatever he gets.*

Having some "liquid" (cash in an interest-bearing money market account) is not a bad idea. How much is determined by debt, which should hover around zero. Neglecting to invest is like the unfaithful servant in the parable of the talents who didn't even get interest on his Lord's money, and was thrown into outer darkness for bad stewardship. Waiting to invest is like waiting to tithe: both should be done early in the Christian life. The goal in living is to live modestly and put God's money to work for him. Learn how to invest, and get started now, even if you can invest only a small amount. Start tithing now at ten percent of your gross. Do it without delay.

You now should have at least a small amount of capital to begin investing with. The goal is to invest in eight different areas (Ecclesiastes 11:2). The pros call it diversification! The bible is specific on the number of initial investments, so you can watch them closely, daily. The stock market, as I said before, runs basically on fear and greed—we as Christians do not run on either. We never invest in anything wrong or harmful, even if the potential return is good; i.e., tobacco products, bad environmental products. Why? Because we are ordered to be stewards of our bodies and our environment.

According to Proverbs:

- 21:5-6 *Steady plodding brings prosperity; hasty speculation brings poverty. Dishonest gain will never last, so why take the risk?*

- 24:3,4 *Any enterprise is built by wise planning, becomes strong through common sense, and profits wonderfully by keeping abreast of the facts.*

- 27:23,24 *Riches can disappear fast. And the king's crown doesn't stay in his family forever – so watch your business interests closely.*

It all starts with respect for God and His creation. We fear Him, and that is a good thing. Fear of God leads to wisdom, knowledge and common sense. We talk to our friends and our wives about any proposed investments: Those who love us and want us to succeed. We know how to spot a fraud because we have read about the character of frauds in the Bible (our investment manual). We also know that good deals are truly a dime a dozen so we are never pressured into a deal! We pray about everything and wait to hear God's voice in his word. We put our trust where it should be, in the Lord. Remember, we have a hidden agenda, to honor the Lord by advancing the cause of righteousness!

We have a lot of freedom in what we invest God's money in, from farming to bio-technology. Be patient. Take it seriously, but have fun with it. Study the markets for your eight investments. If you make a mistake, you still have seven other chances to get it right. Don't hold too tightly to things that aren't working. When you fall, pick yourself up and try again. Stay away from all get-rich-quick schemes. Stay away from multi-market scams by fast-talking high-pressure folks. Think ahead, look ahead, prepare in advance and be cautious. Give it up if it is not working. Do your homework, and watch and learn from others' mistakes. Get all the facts you can. Remember your motive is not to get rich, but to get it right. Commit everything to God through prayer and enjoy the ride. The ride is feeding the poor, helping widows, and orphans by supporting ministries like Vision for peace.org.

According to Proverbs:

• 24:3-4 *Any enterprise is built by wise planning, becomes strong through common sense, and profits wonderfully by keeping abreast of the facts.*

Credit, Debts, and Loans

The old proverb, "He that goes a borrowing goes a sorrowing" should be heeded. There is nothing like debt to bring discouragement in family or business. Debt leads to despair and hopelessness. "The borrower is truly a servant to the lender." If you can't buy it for cash, you don't need it. There will always be those who assure you that a little borrowing is necessary and even prudent, but they are not Scriptural. Heed not their misguided counsel. Better wait and let the deal go by; remember that "good deals" are a dime a dozen. The only debt the Christian businessman should repay on the installment plan is the debt of love. If you are out of debt, stay that way. If you or your business are in debt, get out, the sooner the better. Don't be seduced by silly speeches; you know what I'm telling you is right! Don't borrow or sign a note for friends or family. The Late Larry Burkett said, "The best way to make a distant relative is to loan money to a close one." In business the best way to create strife among your partners is to talk them into debt.

Wise men from the past have made the following remarks, which should be well heeded:

"Never purchase any enjoyment if it cannot be procured without borrowing of others."

"Debt is not an inconvenience, it is a calamity."

121

"Whatever you have, spend less."

"Better to go to bed supper-less, than to rise in debt."

According to Proverbs:

- 22:7b *The borrower is servant to the lender.*
- 3:27, 28 *Don't withhold repayment of your debts. Don't say, "some other time," if you can repay now.*
- 14:15b *A prudent man is cautious and avoids danger.*
- 11:15 *Be sure you know a person well before you vouch for his credit! Better to refuse than to suffer later.*
- 27:13 *The world's poorest credit risk is the man who agrees to pay a stranger's debts.*
- 22:26, 27 *Unless you have the extra cash on hand, don't countersign a note. Why risk everything you own? They'll even take your bed!*
- 17:18 *It's a poor judgment to countersign another's note, to become responsible for his debts.*
- 20:16 *It is risky to make loans to strangers.*

Talking about credit, debts, and loans touches a nerve with everybody. We all have bad memories (or current experience) of the pain and distress unwise financial decisions can bring. Whether through our own ignorance or the incompetence or malice of others, most of us have felt the jaws of a financial bear trap. In my darkest financial times, I prayed a lot, maybe too much, about my financial needs. God has always been faithful, but the pain and anxiety of knowing I couldn't meet certain financial obligations was an extreme emotional burden. Sure, I got myself into the messes I found myself in, but I could have used some help or wise counsel (if I would have listened).

I have never forgotten those desperate days, and therefore try to remember to give as I have been given to. Biblical wisdom tells us to be cautious about our generosity, but we should not be jaded by bad experiences. I have been conned, taken advantage of, stolen from and cheated, but I know it is truly better to give than to receive and that those who have been truly helped are worth all the loss and risk.

Years ago, a street ministry Gordon and I were involved in had a simple rule about money—don't bring any cash you can't afford to lose. Something like that would make a good guideline for giving: give freely to those who have been close enough to earn your trust or whose need is transparently desperate, but give only what you can afford to lose to those whose credibility has not been established..

Real Wealth

There was a true story of a couple who entered the U.S as "boat people." They only had one distant relative in the U.S., an uncle who owned a bakery in a major city. When they arrived, they went to work for this uncle at a joint salary of sixteen thousand dollars per year. They continued their native country's diet, consisting mainly of rice. They washed in the sink, and slept on the flour sacks in the back of the store.

For three years they saved most of their salary and thought that America was great. They had plenty to eat, indoor plumbing, running water from a tap (no more traveling to the local stream), flour sacks on a cement floor in a heated building which had no leaks instead of a dirt – floored hut — America was great! After the three years, they bought the bakery for cash, and now, fifteen years later, they own eighteen more bakeries..

Real wealth is not high living. It is smart living,, careful saving, wise investing, and truly serving and helping others. Most millionaires I know don't drive fancy cars or live extravagant lifestyles. They drive safe, efficient cars and live in regular neighborhoods. They reinvest their money back into their businesses or enterprises. Proverbs validates what I have observed.

According to Proverbs:

- 21:17 *A man who loves pleasure becomes poor.*
- 21:20 *The wise man saves for the future, but the foolish man spends whatever he gets.*
- 22:1 *If you must choose, take a good name rather than great riches; for to be held in loving esteem is better than silver and gold.*
- 11:18 *The evil man gets rich for the moment, but the good man's reward lasts forever.*
- 28:20 *The man who wants to do right will get a rich reward. But the man who wants to get rich quick will quickly fail.*

- 10:7 *Some rich people are poor, some poor people have wealth.*
- 21:17 *A man who loves pleasure becomes poor; wine and luxury are not the way to riches.*

Ingratitude or Thankfulness?

Developing contentment and being grateful is real wealth. The apostle Paul reminds us that Godliness with contentment is great gain. (2 Timothy 6:6) Contentment is built from a grateful heart. Throughout the ages bards and scholars have penned warnings that we should heed concerning ingratitude.

Ungratefulness is the very poison of manhood. – Sir P. Sidney
A grateful dog is better than an ungrateful man. – Saadi
Filial ingratitude! Is it not as this mouth should tear this hand for lifting food to it. – Shakespeare
He that doth public good for multitudes finds few are truly grateful. – Massinger
Brutes leave ingratitude to mark. – Colton
Nothing more detestable does the earth produce than an ungrateful man. – Ausonius
In gratitude; thou marble-hearted fiend, more hideous when thou showest thee in a child; than the sea monster. – Shakespeare
Blow, Blow, though winter wind, thou art not so unkind as man's ingratitude. Freeze, freeze, thou bitter sky, thou dost not bite so nigh, as benefits forget. – Shakespeare
How sharper than a serpent's tooth it is to have a thankless child. – Shakespeare
Not to return one good office for another is inhuman; but to return evil for good is diabolical. – Seneca
An ungrateful man is like a hog under a tree eating acorns, but never looking up to see where they came from. – Timothy Dexter

During WWII General Bradley rebuked General Patton for criticizing one of General Eisenhower's command decisions after General Patton had been reinstated to command the third army. Patton's reply to Bradley, "I'm sorry, I have a lot of faults Brad, but ingratitude is not one of them."

So listen to wise counsel, be a grateful person for whatever God determines to supply, and take nothing for granted. Be thankful and express your thankfulness to God daily as well as to those you work for and with. Without thankfulness and gratefulness life becomes duller and friends become fewer! I Thessalonians 5:18: *Give thanks in every circumstance, for this is God's will for you in Christ Jesus.*

Conclusion

"When all else fails, read the directions." That applies to financial management as well as to putting bicycles together on Christmas Eve. Whether on Wall Street or Main Street, "all else" has shown its capacity for catastrophic failure. We begin to wonder whether the fundamental structures of national or global economy are as sound as we once assumed they were. Economic theories, investment strategies and personal budgets fall by the wayside when their foundations are shaken.

What's the problem? In one word: greed. Corporations and individuals have had their names in the news for mismanagement, poor planning and outright fraud. Everybody wants at least a little more than his or her fair share. Even a "fair share" has come to mean ever-increasing income from secure employment and investments.

The problem isn't new. Jesus never talked about suicide bombers or Super Bowl statistics. Those are interests of our day, but would have had no meaning for the common people who heard Jesus on Galilean hillsides two thousand years ago. Jesus talked about money a lot. Not that He was obsessed with it Himself (He was after all homeless), but it was a topic familiar to his hearers. Jesus tied eternal truth to temporal human concerns. Money has been a human concern since its invention, and concerns about money are just as timely now as they were when the Bible was written.

That's where we can read the directions — in the Bible. The Bible's teachings about money are just as necessary now as they were when people knew the difference between a shekel and a denarius. In good times, even Christians tend to accept secular assumptions about money, and look to the Bible primarily for ethical guidance within the prevailing economic framework. In more uncertain times, we are more likely to see our need to

127

base our whole approach to economics in the teachings of the Bible, and look to secular frameworks primarily for specific applications of biblical truth.

This book does not offer a get-rich-quick scheme, a debt reduction plan or a twelve step program to ensure financial security. It is not about how to succeed in business. It is about how to please God in the way we do business. If the pastor announces a sermon on stewardship, we expect to hear a lot about tithes, offerings and other forms of giving. The Bible teaches about how we earn money as well as what we do with it once we've got it.

Habakkuk's Hope

"Cheer up! Everything's going to be awful!" "If you can keep your head while all around you are losing theirs, you obviously don't understand the situation." Habakkuk understood the situation. Oppression and injustice were ruining his nation. Power and influence were used to exploit the poor and weak. Sound familiar? Habakkuk was surrounded by political, economic, and moral chaos.

When everything goes wrong, the righteous keep going right. But what could Habakkuk do? He prayed. How long will God hold back His judgment? When will He set things right? Will truth and justice be trodden under foot forever? Habakkuk trusted God's character. Surely God's wrath against oppressors and His mercy towards the oppressed would move Him to dramatic action.

God's answer to Habakkuk's cry is astonishing. The bad people will be oppressed by worse people, whose cruelty will overwhelm the whole nation. Where is the justice and mercy in that? God must not be thinking the way Habakkuk is thinking.

Habakkuk's jaw drops, and he blinks in amazement. Then he thinks about it. The real differences in society are not between rich and poor, powerful and weak, or even between bad and good people. The radical difference is between those who trust God and those who trust themselves. Expecting God to look out for our selfish interests is not the deep trust of complete abandonment to His care.

Habakkuk finally gets the picture. Things are bad, and getting worse, "But the Lord is in His holy Temple; let all the earth be silent before him (Habakkuk 2:30)." Governments, economies, and personal fortunes

rise and fall, but God is still God, and He is the only unchanging
foundation for life. What matters is that God is who He is, and we can
know Him and trust Him—whatever happens.

In the day of trouble, Habakkuk trembled at the grim prospects, but
could still say, "Yet I will rejoice in the Lord; I will be happy in the God
of my salvation (Habakkuk 3:18)." His hope was in the Lord. All is not
right with the world, but God is still in His heaven—and in our lives, as
we rest our hope in Him.

From what you have read, you realize that we as
Christians do not claim ownership on anything material. God
gives and, sometimes rather quickly, He takes away. The Apostle
Paul tells us that our job as stewards is to be found faithful
(I Corinthians 4:2) whether the stewardship is in ministry, or
in the financial realm. Faithfulness should be our goal, with an
understanding that God owns all that we have and all that we
are. Our ultimate goal is to glorify God and enjoy Him forever.
Many in business have established the goal of increasing their
personal wealth, forgetting that God makes rich and God makes
poor. When our goal is greed, our god becomes money, which
the apostle makes careful warning of in I Timothy 6:5-19.

"Perverse disputings of men of corrupt minds, and
destitute of the truth, supposing that gain is godliness: from
such withdraw thyself. ⁶But godliness with contentment is great
gain. ⁷For we brought nothing into this world, and it is certain
we can carry nothing out. ⁸And having food and raiment let
us be therewith content. ⁹But they that will be rich fall into
temptation and a snare, and into many foolish and hurtful lusts,
which drown men in destruction and perdition. ¹⁰For the love
of money is the root of all evil: which while some coveted after,
they have erred from the faith, and pierced themselves through
with many sorrows. ¹¹But thou, O man of God, flee these things;
and follow after righteousness, godliness, faith, love, patience,
meekness. ¹²Fight the good fight of faith, lay hold on eternal
life, whereunto thou art also called, and hast professed a good

profession before many witnesses. [13]I give thee charge in the sight of God, who quickeneth all things, and before Christ Jesus, who before Pontius Pilate witnessed a good confession; [14]That thou keep this commandment without spot, unrebukeable, until the appearing of our Lord Jesus Christ: [15]Which in his times he shall show, who is the blessed and only Potentate, the King of kings, and Lord of lords; [16]Who only hath immortality, dwelling in the light which no man can approach unto; whom no man hath seen, nor can see: to whom be honour and power everlasting. Amen. [17]Charge them that are rich in this world, that they be not highminded, nor trust in uncertain riches, but in the living God, who giveth us richly all things to enjoy; [18]That they do good, that they be rich in good works, ready to distribute, willing to communicate; [19]Laying up in store for themselves a good foundation against the time to come, that they may lay hold on eternal life."

With great wealth comes great responsibility. With great wealth comes great temptation, for it is easier for a camel to go through a needle's eye than for a rich man to enter the kingdom of God. Many Christians today have bought the lie that gain is godliness and many are preaching the "prosperity gospel" which indeed is no gospel at all. Their misguided followers, imagining that financial prosperity is an obligation of God and proof of their spirituality, have fallen into the trap of the love of money. Our real wealth is found in doing good and for the rich, it is being rich in good works, ready to distribute and willing to share. Then, what is impossible with men becomes possible because of God's grace; they may lay hold of eternal life.

In business, these principles from Proverbs should be followed because they are right. The Bible is not utilitarian in its application, but rather we as God's people are to follow His principles at all times and in all ages simply because they are His principles. God has absolutely no obligation to His subjects. His moral character and His awesome power demand our respect and obedience in every area that pertains to life and godliness, which includes our finances.

No Christian would doubt the wealth of Christ who said, "Birds of the air have nests; foxes have holes; but the Son of Man has not where to lay His head." For although He had no sure home but Heaven, He was Creator and Sustainer of all. No Christian would doubt the wealth of two of His followers, Peter and John, who when besought by a beggar for money replied, "Silver and gold have I none, but such as I have give I unto you. In the name of Jesus of Nazareth, arise and walk!" For while having no money to give, they gave out of their abundance; the Living Word.

Our true wealth was acquired for us on an old rugged cross, which when applied by faith though accompanied by many trials is "more precious than gold that perishes...," the Apostle Peter reminds us. Through God's adoption of us as sons and daughters, we can now truly say that our Father is independently wealthy! Let us share with others our inherited treasures!

Index

Made in the USA
San Bernardino, CA
30 August 2017